WITHDRAWN

LYRICAL POETRY OF THE NINETEENTH CENTURY

LYRICAL POETRY OF THE NINETEENTH CENTURY

H. J. C. GRIERSON

AMS PRESS
NEW YORK

Reprinted from the edition of 1929, New York
First AMS EDITION published 1970
Manufactured in the United States of America

International Standard Book Number: 0-404-02915-9

Library of Congress Card Catalog Number: 70-124768

AMS PRESS, INC.
NEW YORK, N.Y. 10003

CONTENTS

I. INTRODUCTORY 7

II. EIGHTEENTH-CENTURY LYRIC—BLAKE, WORDSWORTH, AND COLERIDGE . . 19

III. SCOTT, BYRON, SHELLEY, KEATS, AND OTHERS 39

IV. TENNYSON, BROWNING, AND SOME OTHERS . 65

V. ARNOLD AND THE PRE-RAPHAELITE GROUP . 90

VI. "THE NINETIES" 122

LYRICAL POETRY OF THE NINETEENTH CENTURY

I

INTRODUCTORY

To speak on the lyrical poetry of the nineteenth century is, if an interesting, also a difficult task, requiring rather careful and in the end probably incomplete discrimination. For the whole of what is best in nineteenth-century poetry is in essence lyrical—lyrical, not dramatic, not epic. "The true key," says Matthew Arnold, "to how much in our Byron, even in our Wordsworth, is this: that they had their source in a great movement of feeling, not in a great movement of mind." The dichotomy is not quite a sound one. As the Jewish prophets, the Greek tragedians, the poetry and literature of the Renaissance all show, great movements of thought and feeling are intimately connected with one another. It is an inrush of new ideas which quickens the heart and the imagination, and begets the art and literature in which the movement of the mind seeks and finds expression. But in such a movement the feelings may get the upper hand of the judgment, and it is this probably that Arnold meant. In the writings of the prophets, in the tragedies of Aeschylus, in Montaigne and Shakespeare, in Pascal and even Milton, one is conscious of a deeper and fiercer ferment of ideas than one is aware of in any but one or two of the romantic poets, in Goethe, in

Blake, in Wordsworth, in Keats perhaps, but mainly in his letters, and Keats's thought and poetry were only touching maturity when the blind Fury slit "the thin spun Life." The greater body of romantic poetry was inspired by ideas of a rather superficial character or very vaguely conceived:—Byron's mood of passionate protest against everything in heaven and earth; Shelley's dreams of earthly Utopias which are inconceivable and can only be sung about; Scott's buckram mediaevalism, for what is greatest in Scott is all that he has in common with the eighteenth-century novelists—his grasp of the real life and character which underlie all trappings historical or local; Landor's Hellenism; Beddoes' Elizabethanism; and it is hardly necessary to dwell on the still more superficial moods of Moore and Milman and Montgomery and Mrs. Hemans. Nor is it very different with the period that followed. The exquisite art of Tennyson has not disguised to his own age, still less to ours, the comparative poverty of his thought. He feels deeply, and he writes with a wealth of colour and melody that no depreciation can discredit, but he has left no record or interpretation of human nature and human destiny such as can give him a place with the greatest—with Homer or Aeschylus, Lucretius or Virgil or Dante. And Browning, the active and alert-minded Browning, have all his intellectual and metrical gymnastics, his dramatic curiosities, left us with a really deeper impression than Tennyson of life and character? Arnold himself felt the need of ideas in poetry, but into his own poetry he could put nothing but his melancholy. The Pre-Raphaelites abandoned the task and made music and colour and feeling the sole substance of their song. The prophetic mantle of the greater romantic poets—Blake, Wordsworth, Keats—fell not on the poets but on the greater prose-writers of the reign of Queen Victoria—Carlyle, Ruskin, Darwin, Huxley, Arnold, Spencer, Newman.

Now poetry of such a kind, in which feeling predominates, and the shaping ideas are inspiring but vague, will almost necessarily be lyrical or rhapsodical in character; and of this lyrical, subjective, rhapsodical character are all the long poems of the century which count—*The Prelude, Childe Harold, Alastor, Adonais, In Memoriam, Christmas Eve and Easter Day*. Only epic poetry could have given adequate expression to the Greek sense of the heroic, the adventurous, the tragic in human life. Only great tragedy was an adequate medium to present the wrestlings of Aeschylus with the problem of providence and justice. It is in the form, indeed, of lyrical rhapsody that the Jewish prophets utter the deep wrestling of their souls with the revelation of Divine justice and condemnation of evil, but lyric of a kind far removed from song in the ordinary sense of the word. The closest parallel is some of the greater choral odes of Greek tragedy and perhaps some fragments of Blake's *Songs of Innocence* or the *Prophetic Books*, some passages of Wordsworth's *Prelude* or such an outburst in the *Intimations of Immortality* as the stanza—

> Our birth is but a sleep and a forgetting:
> The Soul that riseth with us, our life's Star,
> Hath had elsewhere its setting,
> And cometh from afar,

and both Blake and Wordsworth might not have written quite in this manner but for the example and influence of the Hebrew scriptures. It is in lighter strains that the romantics more often expressed their moods and dreams.

A full and adequate treatment of the lyrical, subjective strain in nineteenth-century poetry would, therefore, have to include a good deal of poetry which is not strictly lyrical in form. It will be wiser to consider what is thus formally lyrical with occasional references to poems like, say, Shelley's *Lines Written among the Euganean Hills* which, though lyrical in character, do not come under the heading of either song or more elaborate ode. We shall accept the Greek classification and confine ourselves to the lyric. "The tact of the Greeks," says Arnold, "in matters of this kind was infallible. We may rely upon it that we shall not improve upon the classification adopted by the Greeks for kinds of poetry; that their categories of epic, dramatic, lyric, and so forth, have a natural propriety and should be adhered to." It was not, however, simply a matter of tact and "natural propriety." The division was determined by the conditions under which each of the kinds named was to be produced,—spoken on the stage; recited, intoned, chanted; sung to the accompaniment of music and, it might be, of dance. Lyric poetry was poetry written to be sung, to be sung on quite definite occasions, for quite definite purposes religious or secular—the Hymn, the Paean, the Hyporchem, the Nome, the Dithyramb, Dirges, and Wedding Songs, nature songs such as the Linos and the song of Adonis. All songs were composed for music, and the greater number for an elaborate dance accompaniment as well. The monodic, subjective lyric of the Lesbian school flourished for only a short time; and this too, though not choral and accom-

panied by dance, was written to be sung: it pre-
supposed a musical accompaniment. "A Greek poet,
it has been said, did not sit down to compose an
Ode to a Skylark or to a Cloud. He wrote, if he were
to serve the Gods, a Hymn, a Dithyramb, a Hyporchem, or the like; or if for men, an Epinicion, a
Threnos, a Wedding-song, or again he gave utterance to his emotions on love, or politics, or on wine
in a Scolion; and in each case he knew that a certain
conformity to customary treatment was expected of
him." The development of lyrical poetry and the
music which accompanied it went hand in hand; and
this was as true of the monodic, personal lyric of the
Lesbian school as of the more elaborate choric poetry
of the Dorian school. Sappho was musician as well
as poet, instructing her disciples in "the arts of music
and rhythm as employed by poetry." Greek lyrics
"were written expressly for song, and the poet in most
cases simultaneously created the accompanying melody. Thus the rhythm of the words indicates exactly that of the music, and as the metre is simple
or involved, regular and stately or abrupt and impet-
uous, such must have been the character of the melody" (Farnell: *Greek Lyric Poetry*, 1891). The
mediaeval lyric of Western Europe, springing from
a root as popular as the Greek, had the same close
dependence on music and dance. What remains of the
popular song, which more courtly elaborations in
Provence and countries which learned from Provence
to a great extent obscured and superseded, breathes
the very spirit of music, as for example the beautiful
Portuguese *cantigas de amigo*. But the more elaborate
courtly songs themselves were written doubtless for
a more elaborate music; and the idea that a song was

intended to be sung was never consciously abandoned
till the end of the seventeenth century. Dryden and
the young courtiers of the Court of Charles II, the
last Court in England which was a focus and inspiration of literature and music and painting, were the last
inheritors of the tradition which dates from the troubadours of Provence.

It is difficult indeed to think that Donne could have
written his songs so heavily weighted with thought and
curious learning with the deliberate intention that they
should be sung. Yet that is still the convention:

> But when I have done so,
> Some man his art and voice to show
> Doth set and sing my pain,
> And by delighting many frees again
> Grief which verse did restrain;

and three of his songs are described in the MSS. as
"made to certain airs which were made before." But
these are the lightest, if any can be called light, of
Donne's songs, and even so, one wonders what a singer
made of them. Some of us may have tried rewriting
the words of an old song and discovered that we had
presented the singer with impossible concatenations of
consonants. No; song and music were parting com-
pany as they had done long ago in Greece after the
highest achievement in the wedding of the two arts
had been attained to in the lyrical passages of the
drama. The poet is content with his own music.

> Heard melodies are sweet but those unheard are sweeter—

and the subtler of the poet's effects elude even the best
reciter. They are

> Felt in the blood, and felt along the heart.

The musician substitutes for them something of his own which may, or may not, be better. "I once asked an eminent musician, the late Madame Goldschmidt, why Shelley's lyrics were ill-adapted to music. She made me read aloud to her the *Song of Pan* and those lovely lines *To the Night*, 'Swiftly walk over the western waves.' Then she pointed out how the verbal melody was intended to be self-sufficient in these lyrics, how full of complicated thoughts and changeful images the verse is, how packed with consonants the words are, how the tone of emotion alters, and how no one melodic phrase could be found to fit the daedal woof of the poetic emotion" (J. A. Symonds: *Essays Speculative and Suggestive*, ii. 251-2).

Yet the original union of song with music and with dance is not to be forgotten and is not forgotten by the poet. Mr. Drinkwater has argued with considerable force that all poetry is lyric, "that what distinguishes other forms of poetry from lyrical is something other than the poetry," that "the characteristic of the lyric is that it is the product of the pure poetic energy unassociated with other energies, and that lyric and poetry are synonymous terms." Metaphysically this is doubtless true. All poetry is poetry. But for my purpose, which is to treat of things as they seem, there is a difference which is recognised by readers, including the makers of anthologies of lyrics which may, or may not, include sonnets but will certainly not include pieces of dramatic, narrative, or argumentative poetry. One feels there is a difference between

> Come unto these yellow sands
> And then take hands

and

> To be or not to be, that is the question,

or even, what is more lyrical in character:

> I know a bank where the wild thyme blows.

What is the difference? The obvious one is the metre. "Once dialogue had come in," says Aristotle, "Nature herself discovered the appropriate measure, for the iambic is of all measures the most colloquial." That is it: "To be or not to be" is *spoken* verse, the lyric is *sung*. It may be, as we have said, that one does not sing it oneself, or wish it to be set to music, none the less one feels that it is intended to be sung. It sings itself. Hence the shorter lines. A trained singer or choir may be taught to sing more elaborate metres. "I know a bank" has been set to music, and similar pieces of as long or longer measures. But simple, natural singing has always required shorter measures because of the necessity of pausing to draw breath. A recent writer on metre (Andersen, *The Laws of Metre*) has argued that the line or couplet of eight feet represents the normal length of what a choir can sing without a definite pause:

> All people that on earth do dwell,
> Sing to the Lord with cheerful voice.
>
> O where hae ye been, Lord Randell my son?
> O where hae ye been, my handsome young man?

There is a sufficient pause to allow of a quick-taken breath at the end of the first line as printed, but the first *real* pause in the sense comes after the eighth foot. From this, the normal English lyrical measure, there are, he states, three main departures, each determined by the distribution and length of the pause. Thus, Common Measure or ballad measure differs from the normal or long measure simply by dropping one foot at the end and so admitting of a longer pause:

> It's narrow, narrow mak' your bed
> And learn to lie your lane; ΛΛ
> For I'm gaun o'er the sea, fair Annie,
> A braw bride to bring hame. ΛΛ
> Wi' her I will get gowd and gear:
> With you I ne'er got nane. ΛΛ

The divisions of the verse consist each of two lines as printed, of seven feet; and the ear is conscious of a longer pause than in the longer measure, one internally beats the interval of a foot. In another variant, the Alexandrine, a foot is dropped, a pause beat out ideally, in the middle and at the end of the line:

When the hour of death is come ∨∨ let none ask whence or why. ∨∨

Most often the Alexandrine is disguised to the eye by the division into two lines frequently with rhyme. Thus Shelley's *Skylark* is really written in Alexandrines throughout and could be printed thus without any other effect than making some of the rhymes what we call internal:

> Higher still and higher from the earth thou springest
> Like a cloud of fire; the blue deep thou wingest;
> And singing still doth soar and soaring ever singest.

There are three clauses, at the end of each of which one expects to pause even if the poet complicates the effect by running on. It is the same with the anapaestic lines in Byron's *Stanzas to Augusta:*

Though the day of my Destiny's over, and the star of my Fate hath declin'd,
Thy soft heart refus'd to discover the faults which so many could find.

A third variant which the author notes is the Nie-

belungen measure in which half a foot is dropped in
the middle and a whole foot at the end of the line:

Thou sayest it I am outcast ∧ : for a God that lacketh mirth. ∧∧

This is not so common, it seems to me, in lyric measures. There are also more exceptional variants where
longer pauses are made or a half-line is inserted among
the full rhythms; but a reader will be surprised to find
how many lyrics whose measures *as printed* seem to
the eye so various are to the ear one or other of the
above or combinations of them.

But I am not writing a treatise on metre. What I
am after is this, that a scrutiny of the *raison d'être* of
the metres we call lyrical bears out what I have said;
one feels—if one has the feeling for poetry at all—
that some poems sing more than others, that we read
them as knowing that these things are sung, not said.
But there are no sharp divisions to be drawn. As the
lines lengthen, as the measures are extended, we still
feel the note of song, even of ecstatic song, "the lyric
cry":

> Our birth is but a sleep and a forgetting;
> The Soul that rises with us, our life's Star
>   Hath had elsewhere its setting,
>   And cometh from afar.

The ode also is song, choric song in origin, but we
feel the difference between its elaborate cadences and
the song that seems to carol in our brains as we read it.
And as we settle down towards narrative and dramatic
verse we draw nearer and nearer to speech. We remain
always above the level of prose speeches, borne on the
wings of verse, but draw nearer to it even when the
speech is impassioned. From blank verse Shakespeare
will pass quite easily into prose, as Shelley in *Prome-*

theus Unbound will glide down from song to blank verse, drawing a little nearer to the ground, submitting what he says a little more to the control of sense and logic.

And this brings me to the last quality of lyric which I wish to keep in view as a differentia, distinguishing lyrical from other forms of poetry, not in kind but in degree. Lyrical poetry, song, took its rise, as the very name indicates, in union with music and dance, and even though the poet no longer writes with music and dance as conceived accompaniment to his words, he yet retains what was the essential motive and effect of the union, the trinity in unity. A good song, even if set to no music and read in silence, still sings and dances in the reader's brain, because it is still an expression of the mood of ecstasy, of escape from the control of reason and prudence and all the routine of life, an escape which in earlier days men and women sought, quite consciously, in song and dance on festival occasions and we in our different way still do. For what music and dance and revel combined does at a lower level and for a larger number, a good lyric—Shelley's *Hymn of Pan*, Keats's *Ode to a Nightingale*, Swinburne's *Itylus* —will still do for the lover of poetry sitting alone in a garret.

The themes of lyric will then be the themes which most readily evoke the ecstatic, the Dionysiac mood. At all times these have been love and wine and revelry and religion and nature as it enters into these experiences, spring for example bringing back the sense of life and the promise of love:

> In the spring time, the only pretty ring time
> When birds do sing, hey ding a ding,
> Sweet lovers love the spring.

The ecstasy of joy and of sorrow, of love and death—
these have been at all times the burden of song, clearly
and simply uttered in the songs of the people, subtilised
and complicated in more courtly and literary poetry.
These are perennial themes; but there have been epochs
when large sections of the human race have been caught
up into an infective mood of ecstasy, as at a religious
revival; and these movements have been of an enduring character, at least in their effects, leaving their record in literature and not least in lyrical poetry. Such
was the effect of the coming of Christianity, and its
lyrical expression is the Greek and Latin hymns. Such
again was the great awakening of the spirit of man in
France and Western Europe at the end of the eleventh
century which gave us the songs of the troubadours
and all that derived from them. Such, too, in a way and
measure, was the period at the end of the eighteenth
century when a variety of causes—literary, political, and
religious—combined to evoke a mood more justly
called lyrical than romantic, the record of which is the
poetry of Blake and Wordsworth and Shelley and
Keats and in a way Scott and Byron, and the successive
phases of which make up the history of poetry in the
nineteenth century. There is, as I have said at the opening of this lecture, a lyrical, rhapsodical vein in much of
this poetry which is not lyrical in form. But much, and
perhaps the best of it, is lyrical in form also, and it is
with this that I propose to deal.

II

EIGHTEENTH-CENTURY LYRIC—BLAKE, WORDSWORTH, AND COLERIDGE

IT is a commonplace of criticism that the eighteenth century was not a period which produced great poetry, was not lyrical in temperament. The age itself was not conscious of the want. For themselves the century seemed, like Pembroke College when Johnson was an undergraduate, "a nest of singing birds," if a more sensitive spirit like Gray's entertained some doubts:

> But not to one in this benighted age
>   Is that diviner inspiration given,
> That burns in Shakespeare's or in Milton's page,
>   The pomp and prodigality of Heav'n.

Songs and odes were produced in abundance. The Miscellanies from Dryden's to Dodsley's are full of them; and a survey of them as represented at their best in Mr. Nichol Smith's *Oxford Book of Eighteenth-Century Verse* will show that in some kinds of lyric, of poems in lyrical form, the poets achieved a certain undeniable level of excellence. There is first the lighter, humorous, epicurean, Horatian lyric of which the century has to its credit a considerable store from the charming songs of Matthew Prior to the graceful occasional verses of William Cowper. There is the reflective, pensive, philosophic lyric of Addison, of Pope (*Ode on Solitude*), Johnson (*On the Death of Mr. Robert Levet*), Akenside, Collins, Gray, Cowper, and others, a kind of lyric destined to live on in the poems of Wordsworth, Byron, Shelley (*The Euganean Hills*),

Arnold, and poets more properly the subject of our consideration. Certain varieties of popular song, as well as the ballad, made appeal to the taste of poets who had no liking for the fantastic or trivial wit of Donne or Cowley or Waller, witness Addison's essays on Wit and on *Chevy Chase;* and Percy and others cultivated these, always a little "to advantage dressed," made more elegant than the popular examples, *e.g.* Gay's

> All in the Downs the fleet was moor'd,

and similar songs and ballads by Tickell and Glover and Cowper. Lastly there was the hymn in which this century, which Carlyle condemned as a howling wilderness of scepticism, is singularly rich. "Our God our help in ages past," "Christians, awake, salute the happy Morn," "Come, O Thou Traveller unknown," "When I survey the wondrous Cross," "How sweet the Name of Jesus sounds," "God moves in a mysterious way," and others, familiar to many who know nothing of their authors, are of this century. They have not the doctrinal range of the Latin hymns. They are strictly Evangelical, their theme the "fountain filled with blood" which cleanses men of their inherited or actual guilt. They have not quite all the passionate quality of the German hymns of the seventeenth century, but they are genuine and moving hymns, not merely pious poems.

What the eighteenth-century lyric in general lacked was the note of ecstasy, the piercing note of joy or sorrow to which we have referred above, the "lyric cry." The poets were too sane. To approximate the confines of pure poetry, to escape from the tyranny of reason, one had to be a little mad—like Collins and

Smart and Cowper and Blake. Only in a hymn could a quite sane poet let himself go, for then he had the sanction of his creed in abjuring reason, *credo quia impossibile,* and the support of a singing, if not dancing, crowd. The preaching of Wesley and Whitfield moved many to ecstasies and hysteria.

But a word of caution is necessary. While I propose to keep this note of ecstasy, the lyric cry which gives wings to the poet's song, always in view, to use it as the final test of lyrical quality, the quality which may determine one to say that a song is more "lyrical" than another which has other qualities, to say that Shelley though not a greater poet than Wordsworth is a greater *lyrical* poet, a more ineffable singer, yet I do not propose to use this test in any exclusive way, to rule out lyrics that have not this quality or have it in a very small measure. As with the distinction between lyrical and other poetry so within the lyrical itself there is nothing to be gained by defining and distinguishing too accurately. Mr. Drinkwater has defined lyrical so precisely that lyrical poetry disappears. I shall be content to take as my guide the form, the use of lyrical measures, or, if the measure used is of an ampler kind, yet the suggestion that the poem, say an ode by Wordsworth, Shelley or Keats, must be inwardly sung or chanted; is not, like dramatic or narrative, spoken verse. In fact I shall take the poet at his word. Who am I to contradict him? My business is to discuss whether he has written a good song or ode or lyrical rhapsody, not to consider too metaphysically whether there is such a thing as a song, an ode, or a lyrical rhapsody.

And it is wise to keep the form as the "Admiral's lanthorn" by which to steer, because the form itself had something to do with the change of the spirit of poetry, the quickening of a more lyrical temper, not all the results of which, one may say, were a gain for poetry. Whatever its limitations of feeling and diction, the elegant or meditative eighteenth-century lyric is often preferable to the fluent, facile, sentimental lyric of which the next century was to produce such an abundance to the delight of our domestic middle-class readers. Poetry begets poetry. The revived interest in our older poetry (not its themes only but the diction and rhythm), the ballad, Elizabethan song, Spenser and Chaucer, the better appreciation of their beauties, dispelled the taste for conventional decoration and dressing to advantage, and, the form reacting upon the temper of poetry, gave us such songs as Blake's

> The wild winds weep,
> And the night is a-cold

and Scott's

> Proud Maisie is in the wood
> Walking so early.

To realise the effect of form upon the spirit of poetry, one need but compare Chatterton's poems in the English of his own day with such poems in his spurious Middle English as

> O sing unto my roundelay,
> O drop the briny tear with me;
> Dance no more at holiday,
> Like a running river be:
>   My love is dead,
>   Gone to his death-bed,
> All under the willow-tree.

But the newer poetry was not altogether a revival of old moods and old modes, though there was to be much of that from Scott's ballads to the virelays and

ballades of Lang and Dobson and Henley. There was
a quickening of the spirit as the eighteenth century
drew to a close in the glooms and splendours of the
French Revolution. There were young men who felt
as Wordsworth describes:

> Bliss was it in that dawn to be alive,
> But to be young was very heaven,

and some of them were poets. If Christopher Smart's
Song of David is the first eighteenth-century song in
which one hears the note of ecstasy, the first great
lyrical poet of the nineteenth century, as I shall reckon
him, though the best and purest of his lyrical poetry
was written before the century began, was William
Blake of the *Poetical Sketches* (1783), *Songs of Innocence* (1789), and *Songs of Experience* (1794). It is
not necessary here, fortunately, to attempt any disen-
tanglement of Blake's philosophy or theosophy. We are
concerned with him only as a singer. But any study
of the songs in these volumes will illustrate the combined influence in a poet of what I have touched on
above; on the one hand, of the literature he has steeped
himself in, as a formative influence, suggesting to him
the forms in which to express himself; and on the
other, the spiritual influence of his own thought and
experience determining what it is he wants to say, the
burden of his song. A poet may be a great artist, like
John Dryden, and yet fail to be quite a great poet if
the substance of his poetry comes to him not from the
impulses and experience of his own soul, but as it
were by order, being the kind of theme for which his
audience asks—and pays. The literary influences in
the *Poetical Sketches* are obvious enough—Elizabethan lyric, the ballad, Macpherson's *Ossian*, the Au-

thorised Version of the Bible, Chatterton, Collins, and
Gray. In the poems other than lyrical the poet oscillates
between the cadence of blank verse and the rhythmical
prose of Macpherson and the Bible. But in the songs
he has learned from the Elizabethans the value of
trochaic and anapaestic rhythms:

> Love and harmony combine,
> And around our souls intwine,
> While thy branches mix with mine,
> And our roots together join.

> The wild winds weep,
> And the night is a-cold;
> Come hither, Sleep,
> And my griefs unfold:
> But lo! the morning peeps
> Over the eastern steeps,
> And the rustling birds of dawn
> The earth do scorn.

He knows, too, that, in song, rhythms can interchange
more readily than in spoken verse, trochee or dactyl
passing into iamb or anapaest:

> Memory, hither come,
> And tune your merry notes:
> And while upon the wind
> Your music floats
> I'll pore upon the stream, etc.

But Blake's songs in *Poetical Sketches* are not of purely
literary inspiration, like the Elizabethan songs of Beddoes. Already in the love-songs and in *A War Song to
Englishmen* we catch a breath of the passionate, troubled experience that will in time put a greater strain
on the lyrical forms than they are quite able to bear.
But the first effect of Blake's realisation of what was to
be the burden of his message in song and prophecy was

to give to his lyrics a new and piercing sweetness. The
memory of childhood and the realisation of its significance for the solution of the mystery of life of
which he was in quest filled Blake's *Songs of Innocence* with an ecstasy of joy such as Thomas
Traherne alone had experienced before him; and
Blake is the better poet. In song after song from the
Introduction,

Piping down a valley wild,

Blake, in iambic, anapaestic, and trochaic rhythms, in
lines variously divided but readily resolvable into one
or other of the units I have described in the first lecture, with some variations, achieves what it is difficult
to describe as anything but perfection, a series of lyrics
quite like which there is nothing else in our language.
The gamut of emotion is not wide; there are regions
of feeling and experience which they do not touch
and which, when Blake came to essay them, were to
trouble his soul and disturb his artistic power to shape
and to control; but within their range, in purity, sweetness, and intensity of feeling, in simple perfection of
diction and variety of rhythm, these songs have no
rivals. Doubtless some are more perfect than others,
at least one or two are a little less perfect—*A Dream*
and *On Another's Sorrow*, which savour a little of
Watts's simple sermon style, with a difference. But to
choose the best among *Holy Thursday, Infant Joy,
Little Lamb,* and others is precarious work. And with
all their simplicity of feeling and diction, these are
metaphysical lyrics. Their inspiration is not the sensuous charm of childhood, but a deeper thought, a passionate faith in the significance of what childhood re-
veals, or seemed to Blake to reveal.

But the very completeness with which Blake entered
into the mind of the child, relived in these poems those
earliest experiences of innocent confidence and happiness, was, one can see, a little ominous. How would he
encounter and control, as man and thinker and poet, the
experiences which adolescence and maturity bring with
them? For most of us as these overtake us childhood
becomes a remote memory. The storms of adolescence
efface it, the chastening effects of experience and re-
sponsibility turn our eyes in other directions—"when
I was a child I thought as a child." Shakespeare remembered little of childhood. His children are little
men. The Elizabethans and the men of the Renaissance
generally laid small stress on childhood. Youth for
them was the beginning of life. Shakespeare's early
plays are the work of a young man, a young Romeo
or Mercutio, a reckless lover and a gay and careless
wit. Then came maturity and manhood, then storm
and stress and disillusionment, and then resignation
and wisdom. Mr. Strachey has justly dispelled some
of the sentimentalism which has invested criticism of
Shakespeare's latest plays. It remains true that the poet
who wrote *The Tempest* towards the end of his life
had outgrown both the illusions of idealism and the
folly of cynicism. He had accepted men as they are,
mixed beings in the mass, neither angels nor devils
but including specimens of both; he had recognised the
inscrutable mystery of life transcending our attempts
to pass judgment on it:

> We are such stuff
> As dreams are made on, and our little life
> Is rounded with a sleep.

And Shakespeare's art as poet and dramatist had

adapted itself and given controlled expression to each
phase in his experience. Even the songs take on a chang-
ing colour, from

> When icicles hang by the wall
> And Dick the shepherd blows his nail,

to

> Fear no more the heat o' the sun
> Nor the furious winter's rages,

and

> Full fathom five thy father lies.

Milton's poetry, too, changed its character with the
vicissitudes through which that bitterly disappointed
but indomitable spirit passed with an unwavering confidence in his own apprehension of truth and justice.
There was a long furrow ploughed between *L'Allegro*
and *Samson*, but both are the works of a great poet.
Now Blake, if one may venture to say it, never quite
grew up, or did so in a somewhat lop-sided fashion.
The child in him would not accept the disillusionment
of experience except on condition that he might
transmute, might sublimate it, and to do so involved
him in a mental conflict the record of which is the
chaotic *Prophetic Books*. His passionate sense of the
innocence and right to happiness of a child would not
accept the inhibitions with which adolescence finds
itself beset, nor the control of the prudence which made
Shakespeare the first burgher in Stratford-on-Avon.

Of the effects of this on his work generally it is not
my business to speak, but one of the first and most
obvious of these effects was on the form of his poetry.
In *The Songs of Experience* one is made aware of the
deepening of thought and feeling in a richer *timbre*,
and the form promises to take an ampler scope:

Hear the voice of the Bard!
Who Present, Past, and Future sees;
    Whose ears have heard
    The Holy Word,
That walk'd among the ancient trees,

Calling the lapsed Soul
And weeping in the evening dew;
    That might control
    The starry pole;
And fallen, fallen light renew!

That has a Miltonic turn and elaboration of period, and

Tyger! Tyger! burning bright,
In the forests of the night

moves with a sterner tread than any of the *Songs of
Innocence*. But the promise was not fulfilled. Few
of the other lyrics show any advance on the metrical
achievement of the first collection; many fall short
of it. From song Blake turned to the free rhythm
of the *Book of Thel*, or the prose of the *Marriage of
Heaven and Hell*, or the rhythm that oscillates between
metre and rhythmical prose of the *Prophetic Books*.
Only occasionally does song re-emerge, and that, when
it achieves excellence at all, is in the mood and mode
of what is best in the *Songs of Experience*, as *The Birds*,
or the great verse in *The Grey Monk*:

For a tear is an ineffectual thing,
And a sigh is the sword of an angel king,
And the bitter groan of a martyr's woe
Is an arrow from the Almighty's bow.

Blake's best lyrics were his earliest. There was no
development of his powers in this direction such as
the lyrics of his greatest successor, Shelley, will reveal.
But Blake's poems were read at the time by no one

who could feel their influence and benefit by it. The predominant influence in English lyric—Scottish song taking a course of its own had already been given a deeper *timbre* and fierier glow from the amazing temperament of Robert Burns—was that of Gray, Collins, and Akenside. The meditative, pensive, elegiac lyric adorned with personifications, as of Contemplation and Virtue, were the vogue and continued to be so for some time after the new century opened. One sees their influence in Coleridge's early verses, even in Byron's *Hours of Idleness*. "The bard who soars to elegise an ass" does so in the traditional manner:

> I hail thee Brother—spite of the fool's scorn!
> And fain would take thee with me, in the Dell
> Of Peace and mild Equality to dwell,
> Where Toil shall call the charmer Health his bride,
> And Laughter tickle Plenty's ribless side,

and Byron himself had delighted in the same elegancies and accepted conventions:

> Repentance plac'd them as before;
>   Forgiveness join'd her gentle name;
> So fair the inscription seem'd once more
>   That Friendship thought it still the same.
>
> Thus might the Record now have been,
>   But, ah, in spite of Hope's endeavour,
> Or Friendship's tears, Pride rush'd between,
>   And blotted out the line for ever.

Wordsworth's two lyrics of 1789 are in the tone and the measure of Collins's *Fidele*. Melancholy, pleasing melancholy, was the dominant mood, and the elegant, restrained style in which the mood might be expressed was stereotyped. Cowper, whose melancholy was sincere and profound, and who knew the value of

simplicity, never in his serious verse (and he is more
often gently gay than serious), lets the feeling quite
break through the convention. The deeper strain is implied rather than expressed:

> You from the flood-controlling steep
>   Saw stretch'd before your view,
> With conscious joy, the threatening deep,
>   No longer such to you.
>
> To me the waves that ceaseless broke
>   Upon the dangerous coast,
> Hoarsely and ominously spoke
>   Of all my treasure lost.
>
> Your sea of troubles you have past,
>   And found the peaceful shore;
> I, tempest-toss'd, and wreck'd at last,
>   Come home to port no more.

And again:

> I therefore purpose not, or dream,
>   Descanting on his fate,
> To give the melancholy theme
>   A more enduring date:
> But misery still delights to trace
> Its semblance in another's case.
>
> No voice divine the storm allay'd,
>   No light propitious shone;
> When, snatch'd from all effectual aid,
>   We perish'd each alone:
> But I beneath a rougher sea,
> And whelm'd in deeper gulfs than he.

The passion rises like a swelling wave, but the wave
does not break. In simple and restrained tones the
poet speaks as it were softly to himself and to those
who have ears to hear. He does not quite sing.

It was through the ballad rather than this dignified
meditative lyric that the spirit of poetry won its way

to a simpler, more poignant diction and a more plangent rhythm. Southey in his ballads made conscious use of the trisyllabic effect which played so important a part in releasing verse from its too regular march, but despite this there is no real music in Southey's ballads. The creators of a new spirit and a finer music were the two poets of the *Lyrical Ballads* of 1798. The title describes, I suppose, what they, or Wordsworth, felt was the effect they were aiming at or had achieved. The poems were to be ballads, not of the heroic, historic type of *Chevy Chase* and *Sir Patrick Spens*, but the simpler, more homely and familiar, even doggerel type, an exceptional example of which, *The Babes in the Wood*, Addison had commended and Wordsworth himself was to cite in the Preface to the 1800 edition—the kind of ballad which had circulated in broadsheets and which, Andrew Lang declared, "in passing through the hands of the printers and poor scholars who prepared them for the press became dull, long-drawn, and didactic." "Dull, long-drawn, and didactic" Wordsworth was willing they should still be, so long as they were simple and sincere. A poem such as *The Thorn* is to be read, he tells us in a note, as the composition of "a captain of a small trading vessel, for example, who, being past the middle age of life, had retired upon an annuity, or small independent income, to some village or country town of which he was not a native, or in which he had not been accustomed to live. Such men, having nothing to do, become credulous and talkative from indolence." But Wordsworth's poems would not have outlived the scorn evoked by his attempts to reproduce dramatically the garrulous style of the broadsheet ballad, if there had not been something more even in some of these

not very happy attempts. Just as dramatic poems put
into the mouth of rustic gossips they are no better
than, if as good as, Southey's *English Eclogues* and
some of his ballads in the same popular style. It is
the something more which Wordsworth adds, sometimes in a single stanza as when in *Simon Lee* after
stanzas about his thick ankles and his aged wife you
are suddenly lifted to a rarer atmosphere:

> I have heard of hearts unkind, kind deeds
>   With coldness still returning;
> Alas! the gratitude of men
>   Hath oftener left me mourning;

and this atmosphere invests the whole of those poems
in which Wordsworth is from the first at his best.
In them even when the theme is still a simple one,
verging even on the ludicrous, the poet is no garrulous
babbler but a singer. The ballad is lyrical:

> You say that two at Conway dwell,
>   And two are gone to sea,
> Yet ye are seven!—I pray you tell,
>   Sweet Maid, how this may be.

But the lyrical inspiration is purest and strongest when
he forgoes the dramatic story altogether and pours
forth in rhapsodical strain his sense of the joyous and
abounding life of nature and its profound significance
for the heart "that watches and receives," as in "I
heard a thousand blended notes," "It is the first mild
day in March," or:

> The eye it cannot choose but see;
>   We cannot bid the ear be still;
> Our bodies feel where'er they be,
>   Against or with our will.

It is with Wordsworth as with Blake. The prophetic and the lyrical inspiration are one in his purest and best songs. It is the joy to which he himself has attained, a mystical, inward joy, that gives intensity and glow and music to his poetry of nature and children and the peasant, especially nature, as the same mystical conviction makes Blake's *Songs of Innocence* more than delightful "namby-pamby." The lyrics of both are dramatic within a certain range—Blake when he puts the song into the mouth of the child:

> Little lamb, who made thee?

Wordsworth successfully so in some of his more tragic lyrical poems, *The Complaint of a Forsaken Indian Woman, The Affliction of Margaret.* But neither poet is ever very far away. He is the interpreter. It is his own innocence Blake rediscovers in the child—for not all young children are little angels—his own passionate affections that Wordsworth utters in *The Affliction of Margaret* or describes in *Michael.* The *Lucy* sequence is really of the same character, a personal experience held at a little distance and dramatically rendered; his affection for his sister contrasted with the passion that had swept him off his feet in France.

In the singing quality of lyric both Blake and Shelley surpass Wordsworth. We are not caught up into the realm of song pure and simple by any of his lyrics as by:

> 'Twas on a Holy Thursday, their innocent faces dear,

or:

> I sang of the dancing stars,
> I sang of the daedal earth.

Wordsworth's lyrical measures are few and simple though he adapts them in a masterly way to his own tune—the ballad or common measure and the fuller octosyllabic or long measure:

> Behold her singing in the field,
> Yon solitary highland lass.

In these, with occasional variations in the stanza form,
he has written all his best lyrical poems, giving to the
measure a certain fulness of meditative passion that
makes the prosody of his songs as distinctive in its
way as that of the seventeenth-century metaphysicals
had been in another way. In neither anapaestic nor
trochaic rhythms is he quite at ease. A song like

> Up with me, up with me into the sky
> For thy song, Lark, is strong

gives one a slightly uneasy suggestion of one trying to
sing with more abandonment than is quite natural to
him. It is in another direction that Wordsworth
widened his compass—that in which Blake failed to
move without letting go metre for cadenced prose—
the direction of ampler and richer measures fitted to
express a greater complexity of feeling, or of thought
and feeling interwoven. In more than one form
Wordsworth did achieve, if always a little unequally,
the form as well as the spirit of the great ode as we
think of that in connection with Pindar and Milton.
There is a movement in this direction in the lyrical
ballads or purer lyrics composed in the decasyllabic line:

> Farewell, farewell the Heart that lives alone,
>   Hous'd in a dream, at distance from the Kind!
> Such happiness, wherever it be known,
>   Is to be pitied; for 'tis surely blind.
>
> But welcome fortitude, and patient cheer,
>   And frequent sight of what is to be borne!
> Such sights, or worse, as are before me here.—
>   Not without hope we suffer and we mourn.

It was in quest of the same effects of exalted, passionate but controlled, meditation that he turned to the
Miltonic sonnet with it sonorous effects; and then
he tried the ode, *Intimations of Immortality* occupying
him from 1803 to 1806. It is in some ways the greatest
of his poems, for in it the pure joy in life and nature,
a joy at once sensuous, organic, and spiritual, of the
earlier short lyrics and of the great rhapsodies of *The
Prelude* becomes the motive of a more sustained, more
elaborately builded lyrical structure at the moment that
the poet is aware that the joy has ebbed, is becoming
a memory, for

> Nature still remembers
> What was so fugitive,

and is for that reason the more eager to give a final
statement of its significance, to supply the rapture of
conversion by a faith in which to live, "a faith that
looks through death." It was a crisis in Wordsworth's
spiritual development on which we need not dwell.
It is somewhat, too, of an epoch in the history of his
art, this effort to rise above simple song, or rhapsody
in blank verse, to a great ode built with the unity and
completeness it was easier to attain in the sonnet.
He does so with a wonderful degree of success but not
without some sense of effort. The building and joint-
ing has cost him trouble. The greatest verses are rhapsodical flights—the first three stanzas, the fifth,

> Our birth is but a sleep and a forgetting,

and the ninth.

Beyond this ode Wordsworth was not to go spiritu-
ally or artistically.

If a great lyrical poet must attain to a certain

grandeur as well as beauty of form such as Dante was in quest of when he chose the canzone because "excellentissima excellentissimis digna sunt," a great theme demands an adequate vesture, the danger attending the statelier forms is that the poet may come to think that they will support themselves. If proof were wanted of the entire sincerity of Milton's artistic inspiration it might be found in the fact that he made no attempt to repeat the splendours of *Paradise Lost* but shaped himself a purer, severer style for the last poems of his old age. Wordsworth failed in this as the inspiration of his first years flagged. His simpler lyrics are empty, his odes pompous, though there were moments of recovery. The lines *Upon the Death of James Hogg* are in the old rhapsodic manner at its best:

> Nor has the rolling year twice measur'd
> From sign to sign its steadfast course,
> Since every mortal power of Coleridge
> Was frozen at its marvellous source,

and I confess to a certain admiration for the stately if a little frigid *Dion*, an ode that owes something to Wordsworth's study of Chiabrera, if it just a *little* reminds one also of Akenside.

The epithet "lyrical" prefixed to "ballads" in the title applies more properly to Wordsworth's contribution than to that of Coleridge, for the latter did not give a new effect to the ballad by making it a vehicle for a new and passionate conviction, the joy of a conversion. He did what Wordsworth failed to do, and in that miracle of miracles, *The Ancient Mariner*, gave to the narrative ballad a dramatic intensity, a beauty of imagery, and a musical subtlety and richness such as it has never known in all its history:

> And now 'tis like all instruments,
> Now like a lonely flute:
> And now it is an angel's song
> That bids the heavens be mute.

All the collectors of ballads, except perhaps Ritson, not least Scott, have dressed them more or less to advantage. The fault of the eighteenth-century dressing was that it was inappropriate dressing, too elegant and dignified:

> Fair Emmeline sighed, fair Emmeline wept,
> And aye her heart was woe:
> At length he seized her lily-white hand
> And down the ladder he drew:
>
> And thrice he clasped her to his breast
> And kist her tenderly:
> The tears that fell from her fair eyes
> Ran like the fountain free.

Even Scott in his early imitations did not altogether escape this sort of adornment:

> For thou from scenes of courtly pride,
> From pleasure's lighter scenes, canst turn,
> To draw oblivion's pall aside,
> And mark the long-forgotten urn.

In the first enthusiasm of his conversion to simplicity Wordsworth was disposed to confound simplicity with clownish awkwardness. Coleridge's finer perception steered him clear of any such rock, though in the first version of *The Ancient Mariner* there are some touches of pseudo-archaism and grotesqueness:

> A gust of wind sterte up behind
> And whistles through his bones;
> Thro' the holes of his eyes and the hole of his mouth
> Half whistles and half groans.

But it was not in this direction, Coleridge quickly felt, that the effect he was in quest of lay. The artistic sophistication of the simple ballad was to be got neither by a studied *simplesse* nor by a studied archaism but by the enhancement of the essential qualities of imagination, dramatic poignancy, and a subtler, sweeter music. It is as though Wordsworth took Coleridge out to the fields to gather daisies and buttercups, and lo! they turned into orchids and exotics at his touch. The language of no ballad could be simpler, more natural, yet there is all the difference in the world between this language and that of prose or the genuinely popular ballad, wherever you take it:

> It ceased; yet still the sails made on
> A pleasant noise till noon,
> A noise like of a hidden brook
> In the leafy month of June,
> That to the sleeping woods all night
> Singeth a quiet tune.

The only obvious enrichment of the ballad-measure which Coleridge allows himself is this addition of a couplet, which is not uncommon in the older ballads, and yet the music is not that of the old ballads itself but something rare and exotic. Coleridge in this ballad is the source of all that the later Pre-Raphaelites, from Keats in *La Belle Dame sans Merci* and some of Tennyson's earliest lyrics to Rossetti and Morris and Swinburne and Oscar Wilde, were to be ever in quest of—the subtle, the exotic. Metrically, and in the suggestion of the magical, *Christabel* and *Kubla Khan* promised more, perhaps, but they remained fragments. Coleridge's refashioning of the ballad is his great and miraculous achievement. But except in the metrical

music of these poems and the one glittering beautiful
song in *Zapoyla*,

> A sunny shaft did I behold,
> From sky to earth it slanted,

Coleridge's poetry is not essentially lyrical. He was
in blank verse and ode a rhapsodiser. *Effusion* is the
name he gives to several of his early pieces, and it is a
good description of most of his pieces outside the three
great things which are dramatic rather than lyrical,
though indeed *Kubla Khan* is the most entranced, the
most musical of his effusions. He lacked the passion,
the intensity of the lyrical poet. The best of his personal poems—*Dejection*, "Friend of the wise," *Time*,
Real and Imaginary, *Youth and Age*—are elegiac effusions, Coleridge's in virtue of their tender, delicate music.

III

SCOTT, BYRON, SHELLEY, KEATS, AND SOME OF THE LESSER ROMANTICS

THE ballad which appealed to Wordsworth as the ideal
expression of the simplicity and sincerity to which he
wished to bring poetry back from "the bracelets, and
snuff-boxes and adulterous trinkets" of poetic diction; which inspired Coleridge's one great dramatic
and imaginatively complete poem; was also the source
of Scott's poems, and so ultimately of the *Waverley
Novels*. But it was not quite the same aspect of the
ballad that "in the summer of 1793 or 1794" quickened
in his mind the long-dormant creative impulse. For
there were three things in the ballad that after the

publication of Percy's *Reliques* appealed variously to different readers: the simplicity, even "flatness or insipidity" (as Scott calls it, for he understood if he did not share Dr. Johnson's attitude) which was Wordsworth's Dalilah; the thrill of the supernatural which the German followers of Percy had specially cultivated and was not without its influence on Coleridge as later on Dante Gabriel Rossetti; and lastly the romantic appeal of love and tragic happenings and "deeds of derring-do." It was with the second of these that Scott began, under the influence of his German studies and of "Monk" Lewis, to whose *Tales of Wonder* (1801) he contributed *Glenfinlas* and *The Eve of St. John.* But the supernatural was not Scott's *forte* except as dramatically handled, seen through a character, as in *Wandering Willie's Tale.* The real Scott emerged in the romantic and historic ballads, whether those he collected and edited (which editing included a great deal of rewriting) in the *Minstrelsy of the Border*, or those which he confessedly composed in imitation. Scott was no purist in the preservation of old ballads. To recover the original ballad, whatever it may have been, was, he knew, impossible; and he did not share Ritson's indignation with Percy because he had "decorated the ancient ballads with the graces of a more refined period"; indeed his own first imitations show a good deal of the same kind of decoration, as in his version of Bürger's *Lenore:*

> Strong love prevailed; she busks, she bounes,
>   She mounts the barb behind,
> And round her darling William's waist
>   Her lily arms she twined.

Cadzow Castle is dignified with the favourite rhetoric of later eighteenth-century poetry:

> But can stern Power with all his vaunt,
>   Or Pomp with all her courtly glare,
> The settled heart of Vengeance daunt,
>   Or change the purpose of Despair?

But Scott knew that this was not the language of the old poets. It is not by such conventional diction that one recognises his hand in the border ballads he edited, but rather by an artistic and temperamental heightening of the romantic and tragic elements which the popularly transmitted ballads often suggest rather than express, or sometimes woefully mishandle. In the older version of *Jamie Telfer in the Fair Dodhead* the description of the fight is in the matter-of-fact style of the popular poet:

> "Fa on them, lads!" can Simmy say;
>   "Fy, fa' on them cruelly!
> For ere they win to the Ritter ford
>   Mony toom saddle there shall be."

> But Simmy was striken o'er the head,
>   And thro' the napskape it is gane,
> And Moscrop made a dolefull rage,
>   When Simmy on the ground lay slain.

> "Fy, lay on them!" co Martin Elliot;
>   "Fy, lay on them cruelly!
> For ere they win to the Kershop ford,
>   Mony toom saddle there shall be."

Scott made his own family, in place of the Elliots, the heroes of the exploit, and his hand is unmistakable in the verses which take the place of those above:

> "Set on them, lads!" quo Willie than;
>   "Fye, lads, set on them cruellie!
> For ere they win to Ritterford,
>   Many a toom saddle there shall be!"

> Then till't they gaed, wi' heart and hand;
>   The blows fell thick as bickering hail;
> And mony a horse ran masterless,
>   And mony a comely cheek was pale!
>
> But Willie was stricken ower the head,
>   And thro' the napskape the sword has gane;
> And Harden grat for very rage,
>   When Willie on the grund lay slain.
>
> But he's tane aff his gude steel cap,
>   And thrice he waved it in the air—
> The Dinlay snaw was ne'er mair white
>   Nor the lyart locks of Harden's hair.

This is no eighteenth-century decoration, but it is *not* the style of the balladists, who do not give us these vivid details and sudden vivid similes. Their similes are few and traditional; their details simple and matter of fact. In such additions as these Scott lends to the ballad his own love of a vivid scene of action and movement, his own dream of the joys of a fight. But Scott is nearer to the spirit of the old singers than Percy and his followers, if he never quite catches the thrill of those occasional verses when the matter-of-fact style of the old ballad lays bare the heart of a dramatic situation:

> O little did my mother think,
>   The day she cradled me,
> What lands I was to travel through,
>   What death I was to dee.

He selects, combines, and improves till it is hard to say how much is his own. It is to Sharpe and Scott, or Scott alone, and to no old balladist that we owe, in all probability, *The Twa Corbies* which carries us back in mind to the oldest traditions of tragic poetry.

It is with Scott's songs as with his ballads. They

are best when they adhere most closely to the spirit
and form of the old impersonal, simple, poignant
folk-song. His few personal lyrics are in the later eighteenth-century manner:

> Though fair her gems of azure hue,
>   Beneath the dew-drop's weight reclining;
> I've seen an eye of lovelier blue,
>   More sweet through wat'ry lustre shining.

"Ah! County Guy," which suggests rather the courtly
than the popular mediaeval lyric, is excellent; but the
greatest of Scott's lyrical flights are the fragments
which poor Madge Wildfire sings on her death, all
good in different kinds,—a song of harvest-home:

> Our work is over—over now,
> The good-man wipes his weary brow,
> The last long wain wends slow away,
> And we are free to sport and play.

A Methodist hymn:

> When the fight of grace is fought,—
> When the marriage vest is wrought.

A "fragment of some old ballad":

> Cauld is my bed, Lord Archibald,
>   And sad my sleep of sorrow;
> But thin sall be as sad and cauld,
>   My fause true-love! to-morrow.

And finest of all:

> Proud Maisie is in the wood,
>   Walking so early;
> Sweet robin sits on the bush
>   Singing so rarely.

"Tell me, thou bonny bird,
  When shall I marry me?"
"When six braw gentlemen
  Kirkward shall carry ye."

"Who makes the bridal-bed,
  Birdie, say truly?"
"The grey-headed sexton
  That delves the grave duly.

"The glow-worm o'er grave and stone
  Shall light thee steady;
The owl from the steeple sing
  'Welcome, proud lady.'"

That and "Fear no more the heat o' the sun" are perhaps the crown of English lyric poetry of the impersonal kind.

Scott's songs, then, the best of them, those which rise above the level of Moore's, and of songs for the drawing-room, or for Edinburgh convivial meetings, are like Blake's earliest songs, like those of Beddoes later, a result of the literary inspiration of the revival. He was not affected by the spiritual agitation which lends a deeper tone to the simplest songs of Wordsworth and Blake. Scott's closest affinity was with the century of Johnson and Fielding and Smollet and Gray. And Byron too, the other great quickener of the romantic movement in Europe, where Wordsworth and Shelley were for long not even names, he too felt and professed homage to the great poetic oratory of Dryden and Pope, for his own temperament was oratorical rather than lyrical. His first songs are of the Collins-Akenside type; even a later, better lyric as "Oh! snatch'd away in Beauty's bloom" is in the same style:

And oft by yon blue gushing stream
Shall Sorrow lean her drooping head,
And feed deep thought with many a dream,
And lingering pause and lightly tread;
Fond wretch! as if her step disturb'd the dead!

Byron found a worse model, for his early attempts, in the facile, sentimental lyric in anapaestic and iambic measures of "the late Thomas Little, Esq.," *i.e.* Thomas Moore. Byron had never the courage to recognise the merits of unpopular poets like Wordsworth and Coleridge (for whose *Christabel* he professed a patronising regard) and later Keats. In his ridiculous "triangular *Gradus ad Parnassum*" he gave the highest place to Scott, followed by Rogers, and thereafter Moore and Campbell; Southey, Wordsworth, and Coleridge standing equal at the bottom. None of those he placed so high was qualified to teach him a purer dialect, a finer music. But Byron had a temperament, and when that began to make itself felt his lyrics, conventional or undistinguished in language and verse, acquire a *timbre* that is all their own. His anapaests in "I enter thy garden of roses," and "The Assyrian came down like the wolf on the fold," and others have a momentum and rush that is unlike the facile ripple of Moore's songs, even the finer but lighter swing of Scott's *Young Lochinvar* and *Bonnie Dundee*. Nor are such lyrics as "There's not a joy the world can give,"

When we two parted
In silence and tears,

or

There be none of Beauty's daughters,

or

She walks in Beauty like the night
Of cloudless climes and starry skies

easily forgotten once they are heard. Their note is
not that of pure, ecstatic song or chant. The tone is
that of the orator, even in song, of one whose words
vibrate with intensity of feeling, but a feeling that
never quite wins through to the magic and music of
perfect expression.

For the greatest singer after Blake among the
Romantics is Shelley. Unlike Blake, his best songs are
not the earliest. He never knew or sang the ecstasy
of joy and innocence as Blake recaptured it in an imaginative interpretation of childhood. Blake's song is
sweeter, his tone more human, but his notes were few;
his voice too soon lost its finest accents, or recovered
them only in occasional snatches. Shelley's song is the
more piercing, and to the end his art is ever growing
finer. The ecstasy that quickens his greatest songs is
not joy, but the ecstasy of sorrow and longing. His
song is sweetest when, like the nightingale, he leans
his breast against a thorn and pours forth his woes and
aspirations. Behind Blake's anger and sorrow is always
the vision, the faith in a joy that will be made perfect:

> Hast thou truly longed for me,
> And am I thus sweet to thee?
> Sorrow now is at an end,
> O my Lover and my Friend.

The Shelleyan note is different:

> I sang of the dancing stars,
>   I sang of the daedal earth,
> And of Heaven and the giant wars,
>   And Love, and Death, and Birth,—
>   And then I changed my pipings,—
> Singing how down the vale of Maenalus
>   I pursued a maiden and clasp'd a reed,
> Gods and men we are all deluded thus!
>   It breaks in our bosom and then we bleed:

but the difference between Blake and Shelley has been so well described by Mr. Arthur Symons, that I shall quote his words because it will save me from much talk about the content of Shelley's lyric: "All his life Shelley was a dreamer, never a visionary. We imagine him, like his Asia on the pinnacle, saying:

> my brain
> Grows dizzy; see'st thou shapes within the mist?

The mist to Shelley was part of what he saw; he never saw anything, in life or art, except through a mist. Blake lived in a continual state of vision, Shelley in a continual state of hallucination. What Blake saw was what Shelley wanted to see; Blake never dreamed, but Shelley never wakened out of that shadow of a dream which was his life." A mistiness of content, the absence of the final vividness of vision, and with all the ardour of his humanitarian feeling a want of the convincing human touch of the verse I have quoted above from Blake, these are the things that must be discounted in Shelley's poetry if one is to enjoy its ineffable music.

For of Shelley's poetry more than that of any of the romantics is Mr. Drinkwater's *dictum* true, that all poetry is lyrical. In two longer poems, following Hunt and Byron, he essayed to talk in verse—*Julian and Maddalo* and the *Letter to Maria Gisborne*; and not here alone but also, though this has not been emphasised, in some of his last most intimate lyrics—"Do you not hear the Aziola cry?", "The Serpent is shut out from Paradise," "Now the last day of many days," "Ariel to Miranda." These are in the tone of one who talks in gentle, winning accents. But even Shelley's talk is winged. The albatross moves across the deck but his wings support his steps. *Julian and Maddalo* "is Byron and fire," Mr. Symons says—an ethereal fire, a rarer music. Elsewhere, if we set aside deliberate experiments in a manner that was not his own, as *The Cenci* and some satires, his voice is that of the rhapsodist when it is not that of the singer "pinnacled dim in the intense inane." *Alastor* (1816) is a continuous rhapsody in a blank verse more sustainedly musical than Wordsworth's, if *Tintern Abbey* and the greatest rhapsodical passages of *The Prelude* are clearer in imaginative vision and touch a deeper chord of feeling. If Wordsworth's rhapsodies can give place to prosaic preachifying, Shelley's can, and do at times in *The Revolt of Islam* and even the finer, if very unequal, *Prometheus Unbound*, pass into shrill declamation, just as his voice, musical in reading poetry, grew harsh and discordant when he argued excitedly. But Shelley in his greatest poems rises above both rhapsody and declamation to song, whether elaborate song, resembling in sustained and varied harmony, if not in detail of form, "those magnific odes and hymns wherein Pindarus and Callimachus are in most things worthy," or the simpler, more piercing strains of his shorter lyrics which in musical quality have no rival.

In the first class I would place the *Lines Written among the Euganean Hills* (1818), in which Shelley seems to me to rise above the shifting rhapsody of *Alastor* to a sustained song, an ode with a suggestion of Milton's architectonic art; *Epipsychidion*, which climbs from moment to moment of ecstatic feeling to culminate in the glowing description of the ideal island of retreat:

> Famine or Blight,
> Pestilence, War, and Earthquake never light

Upon its mountain peaks; blind vultures, they
Sail onward far upon their fatal way:
The winged storms, chanting their thunder-psalm
To other lands, leave azure chasms of calm
Over this isle, or weep themselves in dew,
From which its fields and woods ever renew
Their green and golden immortality.
And from the sea there rise, and from the sky
There fall clear exhalations, soft and bright,
Veil after veil, each hiding some delight,
Which Sun or Moon or Zephyr draw aside,
Till the isle's beauty, like a naked bride
Glowing at once with love and loveliness,
Blushes and trembles at its own excess.

Lastly, there is *Adonais*, the greatest of these sustained lyrics, a poem in which Shelley's sense of something amiss in the nature of things finds its fullest expression when he discovers that kings and priests and all the other ills that flesh is heir to are but shadows of one radical evil—finite life; that death is the portal through which we escape or return to

That Benediction which the eclipsing Curse
Of birth can quench not.

In each of these poems he has used a different measure and to each has given its fullest lyrical quality.

Next to these in compass and elevation come more formal odes as the *Hymn to Intellectual Beauty*, *To Constantia, Singing*, the *Ode to the West Wind* whose volume and vehemence raise it to the level of *Adonais*, and the greater choral parts of *Prometheus* and yet more of *Hellas*, for allowing all their poignancy and beauty to the lyrics in the first act of the former, those of the third and fourth act seem to me too void of vision and content. Not all the rapture of Shelley's rhymes can compensate for the absence of any such vision as

Dante's *Paradiso* affords. It is a tale of little meaning though the words are strong, and the feeling fervent.

There remain the lyrics, and the fragments of lyrics, pure and simple, in which Shelley pours forth all the ecstasy of his personal sorrows and joys. Here Shelley sings indeed with no suggestion of declamation or chanting. The lyrical measures set him free to utter what he desires or imagines, unhampered by logic or narrative. He was strangely slow in discovering his own powers. The first unmistakably Shelleyan lyric is the stanzas of April 1814:

> Away! the moor is dark beneath the moon,
>   Rapid clouds have drunk the last pale beam of even:
> Away! the gathering winds will call the darkness soon,
>   And profoundest midnight shroud the serene lights of heaven.

In that he masters for the first time the possibilities of the free accentual foot of English verse of which he is to employ almost every possible variety—iambic, anapaestic, trochaic, dactylic—understanding also how within the same song or verse one may pass from trochaic or dactylic to anapaestic and iambic effects:

> Swiftly walk | over the | Western | waves,
>   Spirit of | Night
> Out of the | misty | eastern | caves,
> Where all | the long | and lone | daylight
> Thou wov|est dreams | of joy | and fear,
> Which make | thee ter|rible | and dear,—
>   Swift | be thy flight.

But that belongs to 1821. Before it had come, in 1815, "We are as clouds that veil the midnight moon,"

and "The wind has swept from the wide atmosphere";
and in the same year:

> The cold earth slept below,
>   Above the cold sky shone;
> And all around, with a chilling sound,
> From caves of ice and fields of snow,
> The breath of night like death did flow
>   Beneath the sinking moon,

the piercing tone of which is heightened by the art
of the stanza and the echoing rhymes. One gets the
same effect in 1817 in:

> That time is dead for ever, child!
> Drowned, frozen, dead for ever!
>   We look on the past
>   And stare aghast
> At the spectres wailing, pale and ghast,
> Of hopes which thou and I beguiled
>   To death on life's dark river.

Shelley, like Donne in the *Songs and Sonets*, is prolific
of emotionally effective stanza forms. To 1818, for
example, belong both:

> Come, be happy!—Sit by me,
> Shadow-vested Misery:
> Coy, unwilling, silent bride,
> Mourning in thy robe of pride,
> Desolation—deified!

and the wonderful lyrical transformation of the Spen-
serian stanza in:

> The sun is warm, the sky is clear,
> The waves are dancing fast and bright,
> Blue isles and snowy mountains wear
> The purple noon's transparent might,
> The breath of the moist earth is light,

> Around its unexpanded buds;
> Like many a voice of one delight,
> The winds, the birds, the ocean floods,
> The City's voice itself, is soft like Solitude's.

In 1819, if he tries his hand at simpler, more popular measures in some of the political poems, he is all himself in:

> Arise, arise, arise!
> There is blood on the earth that denies ye bread;
> Be your wounds like eyes
> To weep for the dead, the dead, the dead.
> What other grief were it just to pay?
> Your sons, your wives, your brethren, were they;
> Who said they were slain on the battle day?

To the same year belong besides *The West Wind*, both "I arise from dreams of thee" and "The fountains mingle with the river" as well as some lovely fragments. But 1820 is the culminating year of Shelley's more ecstatic lyrics—his nature lyrics, *The Sensitive Plant*, *The Cloud*, *To a Skylark*, *Autumn: A Dirge*, *The Question*, all less interesting as transcripts of nature than as musical utterances of Shelley's own dreams and desires. To the same year belong the stately *Hymn of Apollo* and the more bewitching *Hymn of Pan*, the most surprising and delighting of Shelley's stanzas, and perhaps the greatest of his lyrics in virtue of the sudden transition in the last stanza from a Bacchic ecstasy to an all-too-human sorrow. And these are only some of the shorter poems of this year, which was also the year of *The Witch of Atlas* and *Adonais*.

In 1821 I seem to note a slight change of tone in Shelley's lyrics. *Epipsychidion* indeed is in the most ecstatic vein; but the predominant note is that of a piercing, yet a more resigned and controlled, sorrow:

"Orphan Hours, the Year is dead," "Swiftly walk over the western wave,"

> Far, far away, O ye
> Halcyons of Memory,

> Rarely, rarely, comest thou,
>   Spirit of Delight,

> O World! O Life! O Time!
> On whose last steps I climb,
> Trembling at that where I had stood before;
> When will return the glory of your prime?
> No more—Oh, never more.

In the love-songs inspired by Jane Williams the tone of the singer blends with that of one who holds a woman's hand and talks in gentle, winning accents:

> One word is too often profaned
> For me to profane it,

> Do you not hear the Aziola cry?

> The serpent is shut out from Paradise,

> When the lamp is shattered
> The light in the dust lies dead,

and *To Jane: The Recollection*, that delicate record of a day of "peace in Shelley's mind."

I confess that these lyrics, saturated with the poet's own personality, appeal to me more than the ecstatic but somewhat empty lyrics in which the coming of a golden age is celebrated in *Prometheus Unbound*. If the choruses of *Hellas* are greater than those of the more ambitious poem it is partly that their art is richer, more starry, and because they are more deeply weighted with the poet's sense of sorrow and a hope akin to despair. All Shelley's heart pours itself out in the final song:

> The world's great age begins anew.

Whatever men may think or come to think of the worth of Shelley as a thinker and prophet, his place as a singer, as a lyrical poet *par excellence,* could only be challenged if our whole prosody underwent some change that made the music of his rhythms and rhymes and patterns of sound no longer fully intelligible. If nevertheless one finds oneself preferring some of the lyrics or odes of Blake and Wordsworth, it is only because the feeling they communicate is, or seems to be, of more general and more enduring, more life-giving worth.

The lyric measures, in which Shelley achieved his most indubitable successes, and is most purely, uniquely himself, did not make the same appeal to Keats's less soaring and ardent, more meditative, more luxurious temperament, loving to "load every rift with ore" —the ore of sensuous, felicitous epithets and richly cadenced rhythms. His one good song, "In a drear-nighted December," he owes to Dryden, but in the first two verses surpasses his original. He wrote one great ballad, *La Belle Dame sans Merci,* with the magic of Coleridge and a more passionate flow:

> I saw their starv'd lips in the gloam
> With horrid warning gaped wide,
> And I awoke, and found me here
> On the cold hill's side.

His trochaic musings in *Fancy,* "Bards of Passion and of Mirth," "Souls of Poets dead and gone," "No, those

days are gone away," are delightful poems, worth
comparing with Shelley's *Euganean Hills*. Keats's
visionary scenes are the more concrete and vivid,
Shelley's the more atmospheric; and if Shelley's music
is the more plangent, Keats's lighter handling has an
Elizabethan mellowness and charm, nor does it lack
a genuine lyrical note:

> Where the daisies are rose-scented,
> And the rose herself has got
> Perfume which on earth is not;
> Where the nightingale doth sing
> Not a senseless, tranced thing,
> But divine melodious truth.

But the ode, not the lyric, was to be the field of Keats's
triumph over all his contemporaries. Dryden's and
Gray's odes are brilliant achievements in the artificial
and rhetorical; Wordsworth's *Intimations* is a great
poem, but an unequal ode; Shelley's odes, expressly
so called, and on an elaborate scale—*Ode to Liberty*
and *Ode to Naples*—are failures; there are, it seems to
me, just two odes entirely satisfying in imagination,
evolution, and music ("echoing and ringing with
music") before Keats, and those are Spenser's *Epi-
thalamion* and Milton's *Lycidas*. To these Keats has
added *Ode to a Nightingale, To Autumn, Ode on a
Grecian Urn*, and, on a slightly lower level of elaboration or perfection, *Ode on Melancholy, Ode to Psyche*.
I put the three I have named first because there is
more in them of the subtle and elaborate evolution
of a thought, or a train of thought, which is the chief
distinction between an ode and a song on the one
hand, an ode and a sonnet on the other. The *Ode on
Melancholy* reads to me like an expanded sonnet, the

statement of a single complete thought. The ode *To
Autumn* is not longer—three stanzas—but it carries
one, not only from one phase of an emotional mood to
another, but from autumn at the close of summer to
autumn trembling on the verge of winter. The *Ode
on a Grecian Urn* has the same movement from an
opening to a closing thought. It seems to me the
greatest "stroke of invention," as Addison might have
called it, the most surprising and yet convincing approach to its subject, which is the perennial value of
beauty. The Attic shape "teases" the poet "out of
thought," suspends the critical judgment "as doth
eternity," so that the work of art, the cold pastoral
of the urn, becomes a moment of warm life "for ever
new," of love

> For ever warm and still to be enjoy'd,
> For ever panting and for ever young.

In the last stanza, as in that of the *Nightingale*, the
vision fades, thought is resumed, but the urn remains
to renew such an illusion from generation to generation,
a witness of the eternity, the supreme value, of beauty.
The *Ode to Psyche* is in a looser structure of stanza.
It has some of the same originality of conception, if
that conception is vaguer; and it is hardly less rich in
imagery than any of the five. I find it hard to think
with Mr. Garrod that the Love for whom the casement
is "ope at night" can be Psyche and not Eros.

   Sonnet and ode, these are Keats's favourite lyric
forms, not song; and he has written some fine sonnets,
but it was in the odes that the full current of his soul,
his deep sense of the beauty of nature, the significance
of art and mythology as the symbols in which the
human soul had sought to give expression to its adum-

brations of the true values in nature and man, his impassioned sense of the fundamental mystery of beauty, fleeting yet perennial, was given richest and most harmonious expression.

To attempt in a short lecture a survey of all the poetry in lyrical form produced during the first quarter or half of the century would be a waste of time and space. As has been already said, the later eighteenth-century lyric of the Collins-Akenside tradition had a certain dignity of tone and form. If somewhat frigid, it is less sentimental and facile than the lyrics in which the magazines of the early century abounded, by popular poets enjoying a reputation far superior to that of Shelley or Keats—Moore, Campbell, Mrs. Hemans, James Montgomery, David Macbeth Moir, Barry Cornwall, and many another. The influences that inspired in different ways the poetry of Wordsworth and Coleridge and Byron and Shelley, and the influence of the first and third of these poets in turn, tended to encourage an effusion of lyrics, simple without a deeper significance, turbulent without passion, making when the theme is domestic "an almost indecent assault upon the emotions."   All that need be said has been said about Moore's light jingle, and Campbell's two or three brilliant achievements in the oratorical lyric. *The Battle of the Baltic* is the finest metrically, a dignified oratorical stanza which perhaps owes something in its original form to Cowper's *Loss of the Royal George*, but in its final elaboration was unique as a stanza suitable for a stately ode, whose influence is perceptible in Tennyson's *The Revenge* and Browning's *Hervé Riel*. But *Hohenlinden* has a more lyrical impetus if also oratorical.

Such space as I have, however, must be given to
poets whose inspiration and art are genuinely lyrical,
not merely such as have written poems in lyrical form.
Of such, contemporaries of the greater poets already
touched on, Walter Savage Landor stands by himself
a little as Robert Herrick does in the seventeenth century. Both wrote epigrams, and in truth the majority
of their lyrics, even the most beautiful of them, are
more akin to the epigrams of the kind in the Greek
Anthology than to song passionate and musical like
that of Burns or Blake or Scott or Shelley. They are
exquisite carvers of cameos, or heads upon cherry-
stones, if Herrick is the more delightful because more
natural, less pretentious. No one can excel Landor
in saying nothing in a stately way whether in prose
or verse; and one can grow tired of it, of expecting
to be more interested and moved than one ever is.
"Coldness," Landor tells us, "is experienced in the
highest beauty. . . . Where there is great regularity
of feature I have often remarked a correspondent
regularity in the affections and the conduct." The
comment could be well illustrated from his own poems;
but "Tanagra, think not I forget" is a fine ode in the
Akenside manner, and in "Rose Aylmer" he has, after
some experiments, caught the tone of passion, but the
lyric cry, the note of ecstasy, is never Landor's. I
confess to preferring to all his shorter poems the
equally classical grace and the greater lyrical vitality
of the songs which Peacock, like Landor, scatters
through his prose. *The Death of Philemon* is such a
ballad as Landor might have written but never did;
and in an utterly different vein of feeling Peacock's
lyrics have something of the originality and purity of
Shelley's: "I play'd with you 'mid cowslips blowing,"

"Seamen three! What men be ye?", "I dug beneath the cypress shade," " 'Tis said the rose is Love's own flower," "By the mossy weed-flower'd column." Even the humorous songs are genuine lyrics—"In the last binn Sir Peter lies":

> None better knew the feast to sway,
>   Or keep Mirth's boat in better trim;
> For Nature had but little clay
>   Like that of which she moulded him,

and *The War-song of Dinas Vawr:*

> The mountain sheep are sweeter
>   But the valley sheep are fatter,
> We therefore deemed it meeter
>   To carry off the latter.

Peacock communicates the delight which his wit afforded to himself. His verse gives it wings.

A genuine, original, musical vein of lyrical poetry is also unmistakably present in the best songs of a very different poet, the peasant John Clare. The interest which Clare's first volume, *Poems Descriptive of Rural Life and Scenery* (1820), excited was due in part to the fame of Burns, and he follows Burns occasionally in choice of subject and manner, never with much success. His genius was entirely different. He had neither the passionate temperament of Burns nor the powerful mind which made him the equal in conversation of the most cultured ornaments of Edinburgh society. Clare was more akin to Shelley than to Burns, not the philosophical and revolutionary Shelley but the sensitive Shelley craving for human sympathy and turning to nature for consolation:

Away, away from men and towns,
To the wild wood and the downs—
To the silent wilderness
Where the soul need not repress
Its music lest it should not find
An echo in another mind.

Clare's *Address to Plenty* is composed in the same measure as Shelley's *Lines Written among the Euganean
Hills,* and both poems are the expression of a poet's
sorrow, his longing for the rare moment of happiness:

Many a green isle needs must be
In the deep wide sea of Misery,
Or the mariner worn and wan
Never thus could voyage on,

or, in Clare's lines:

O thou Bliss to riches known,
Stranger to the poor alone;
Giving most where none's requir'd,
Leaving none where most's desir'd.

But Clare knows, as Shelley did *not,* what would give
him happiness—release from poverty:

Oh, sad sons of Poverty
Victims doom'd to misery;
Who can paint what pain prevails
O'er that heart which Want assails?
Modest shame the pain conceals:
No one knows but he who feels.

The poem ends in a blissful contemplation of the joy
of relief from care:

Oh, how blest amid those charms
I should bask in Fortune's arms,
Who defying every frown
Hugs me on her downy breast,
Bids my head lie easy down,
And on winter's ruins rest.

> So upon the troubled sea,
> Emblematic simile,
> Birds are known to sit secure,
> While the billows roar and rave,
> Slumbering in their safety sure,
> Rock'd to sleep upon the wave.

If Clare's poem lacks the atmospheric splendours and the prophetic tones of Shelley's, it seems to me the expression, and adequate expression, of a mind equally sincere and sensitive, and his management of this measure, so well suited for meditative rhapsody, is hardly less musical. And poignancy is the note of all Clare's best poems, whether the feeling be love of nature or personal sorrow. Clare loved nature with more of knowledge than Shelley, with less of illusion than Wordsworth. Keats was not wrong, perhaps, in saying of the poem *Solitude* "that the description too much prevailed over the sentiment," yet a careful reader will feel that for Clare the details are not mere description, his imagination broods so fondly over each; and so it is in simpler lyrics as *Song's Eternity:*

> What is song's eternity?
>   Come and see.
> Can it noise and bustle be?
>   Come and see.
> Praises sung or praises said,
>   Can it be?
> Wait awhile and these are dead—
>   Sigh, sigh;
> Be they high or lowly bred
>   They die.
>
>   .   .   .   .   .
>
> Dreamers mark the honey-bee;
>   Mark the tree
> Where the blue-cap "tootle tee"
>   Sings a glee

Sung to Adam and to Eve,
    Here they be.
When floods covered every bough,
    Noah's ark
Heard that ballad singing now,
    Hark, hark.

In dealing with the lyrics of the nineteenth century I
shall have to touch on, or pass over, many fine mocking-
birds, poets who catch with singular skill the tone and
music of the lyrics of the greater poets of the day,
yet are *not* great lyrical poets. Clare's is an authentic
voice, if it has not many notes, perhaps only two—this
deep love of nature, and an accent of hopeless sorrow
as piercing as Shelley's, if more subdued; for example:

Love lies beyond
The tomb, the earth, which fades like dew,
    I love the fond,
The faithful, and the true, etc.,

and

I am; yet what I am none cares to know,
    My friends forsake me like a memory lost;
I am the self-consumer of my woes,
    They rise and vanish in oblivious host,
Like shades in love and death's oblivion lost;
And yet I am and live with shadows, tost

Into the nothingness of scorn and noise,
    Into the living sea of waking dreams,
Where there is neither sense of life nor joys,
    But the vast shipwreck of my life's esteems;
And e'en the dearest—that I loved the best—
Are strange—nay, rather, stranger than the rest.

I long for scenes where man has never trod;
    A place where woman never smil'd or wept;
There to abide with my Creator, God,
    And sleep as I in childhood sweetly slept:

> Untroubling and untroubled where I lie;
> The grass below—above the vaulted sky.

Clare's natural, at moments piercing, note is the antithesis to the exotic lyrics of Thomas Beddoes. Of exotics the nineteenth-century poets, exploring all the regions of older or foreign literature, are to produce not a few, but perhaps none are so entirely exotic as Beddoes' plays in the Elizabethan manner, and songs modelled on the Elizabethan lyric, and on some of the shorter snatches of Shelley as "Music, when soft voices die" and

> False friend, wilt thou smile or weep
> When my life is laid asleep?

Beddoes essays both the sombre and the grotesque lyric after the manner of Webster's

> Hark now everything is still.

His own morbid temperament contributed its share to the peculiar effect he arrived at, but his successes are in lines and stanzas rather than in whole poems. The first stanza of the *Dirge for Wolfram* is Beddoes at his best:

> If thou wilt ease thine heart
> Of love and all its smart,
>   Then sleep, dear, sleep;
> And not a sorrow
> Hang any tear on your eyelashes;
>   Lie still and deep,
> Sad soul, until the sea-wave washes
> The rim o' the sun to-morrow,
>   In eastern sky.

In the same way the first two verses of "If there were dreams to sell" make a perfect lyric to which the three that follow add nothing. The interest and importance of Beddoes is that his deliberate artistry (a disagreeable word but almost unavoidable in speaking of Beddoes), his studied rhythms and stanzas, were indicative of one main direction in which the lyric was to develop. The simple, straightforward song of Blake, of Wordsworth, of Shelley too, though his rhythms and stanzas are more varied, had been given by these poets such a fulness of inspiration and music that it was difficult for a successor to write even a fairly happy song, as Hood, for example, in "Fair Inez," or "We watch'd her breathing through the night," that gives the impression of more than a good minor poem. What a poet might still do was to give a comparatively simple measure a new weight of thought, a more metaphysical cast, as Clough occasionally and Arnold were to do, or, like Beddoes but with more of poetic force and variety, cultivate a subtler, a more exotic art. These, it seems to me, are to be the two tendencies of the Victorian and post-Victorian lyric, blended to some degree in almost all the greater poets, but with the one or the other, the metaphysical or the virtuoso, predominating in this or that poet—the virtuoso in Tennyson, Rossetti, Morris, Swinburne, Lang, Henley, Dobson, Wilde, Kipling; the metaphysical in Clough, Arnold, Meredith, Patmore (to leave out Bailey and Horne), Newman. In Browning the virtuoso and the metaphysical are blended in such a strange way that he has received more than his due as an original thinker and much less than his due as a bold experimenter and astonishing virtuoso. In the *Odes* of Francis Thompson also the two strains are essayed and combined with more of ambition than of entire success.

IV

TENNYSON, BROWNING, AND SOME OTHERS

THE simple, sentimental lyric had abundant vogue during the years when, it must be remembered, Shelley and Keats were still undiscovered, and their great successors, the Dioscuri of the earlier Victorian age, were only making their slow way to recognition and popularity. Mrs. Hemans, L. E. L., Thomas Haynes Bailey, Robert Montgomery, and others represent, better than the greater poets, the taste of the early Victorian age,—middle-class, pious, sentimental. A study of their work belongs rather to social than to literary history. It was against poetry of this bourgeois, sentimental kind in Holland that a number of young men in the eighties made a vehement protest, declaring that poetry was not sentiment and sermons but art and passion. We were more fortunate in the possession of great poets whose work, as it gradually made itself felt, dispelled the influence of this inferior stuff without the necessity of an active crusade and the foundation of such a periodical as *De Nieuwe Gids* to make the appeal effective. Yet it is well to recall what was the taste of the period in poetry as in other things, for the poet who wrote *Lady Clara Vere de Vere* and *The May Queen* made throughout his life concessions to the taste of his audience, and so in his way did the less popular author of *Pippa Passes* and *The Blot in the 'Scutcheon* and *Colombe's Birthday*, and, shall we say, even *The Ring and the Book*; and Mrs. Browning and the "Spasmodics," Smith and

Dobell, were more gifted and artistic representatives of the same taste for the sentimental and edifying. Unless we remember this we shall fail to understand the revolt in the sixties of Arnold and Rossetti and Morris and Swinburne and others against the taste poetic and artistic of their age. Tennyson and Browning could be sentimental in a way that to some readers is as trying as the *simplesse*, the "silly sooth," of Wordsworth or the occasional vulgarity of Keats.

But indeed, until we disengage ourselves from the impression of Tennyson and Browning as great philosophical poets, which was the conviction of their later admirers, we shall fail to do justice to what they both undoubtedly were—very great and cunning artists in very different yet complementary ways, who enriched the whole compass of English poetry and not least the lyrical poetry which they took over from their more passionately inspired predecessors.

The younger Tennyson of the successive volumes—*Poems, Chiefly Lyrical* (1830), *Poems* (1833), and *Poems. By Alfred Tennyson. 2 vols.* (1842)—was not burdened by any such message as inspired the lyrics of Blake and Wordsworth, nor were his early songs the vehicle of any such intense personal feeling as Shelley's songs had been from the time he wrote "Away, the moor is dark" to the last *Dirge* he composed:

> Rough wind that moanest loud,
>   Grief too sad for song;
> Wild wind, when sullen cloud
>   Knells all the night long;
> Sad storm whose tears are vain,
> Bare woods whose branches strain,
> Deep caves and dreary main—
>   Wail for the world's wrong.

When Tennyson expresses his personal feelings his tone, both now and later, is inclined to be a little hysterical. He is happiest as the artist, interested in the perfect expression of some single, intense mood dramatically conceived, for Tennyson anticipated Browning in the cultivation of what the latter called Dramatic Lyrics and Dramatic Idylls, if Tennyson is concerned mainly with a single mood and its adequate rendering in word and image and rhythm, less eager to suggest shades of character individual or historical, and less dialectical. The successive revisions which Tennyson's poems underwent show with what care he labored to achieve his aim, the rendering of a mood, by the selection and the ordering of the picturesque details, by the choice of emotionally significant detail, and the subtle varying of the cadences. It is of Beddoes rather than the greater romantics that Tennyson's artful cadences remind a reader, the Beddoes of "If there were dreams to sell" and such lovely cadences as:

> We have bathed where none have seen us,
> In the lake and in the fountain,
> Underneath the charmed statue
> Of the timid bending Venus, etc.

But Beddoes' moods are few, his art laboured. Tennyson's 1842 volumes are a series of masterpieces in the picturesque and metrical rendering of moods and dreams: "Where Claribel low lieth,"

> Eyes not down dropt nor over-bright, but fed
> With the clear-pointed flame of chastity,

the *Mariana* poems, *The Arabian Nights*, "A spirit haunts the year's last hours," *The Dying Swan*,

"Now is done thy long day's work," the wonderful
flow and the chiming rhymes of the *Lady of Shalott*,
to say nothing of its dramatic poignancy:

> All in the blue unclouded weather
> Thick-jewell'd shone the saddle-leather,
> The helmet and the helmet feather
> Burn'd like one burning flame together,
>   As he rode down to Camelot,
> As often through the purple night,
> Below the starry clusters bright,
> Some bearded meteor trailing light,
>   Moves over still Shalott.

Add to these *The Lotos-Eaters* with its closing chorus,
and the varying rhythms of *The Vision of Sin*. One
may prefer to these rich and manifold cadences song
which, like that of Burns or Blake or Shelley, flows
more directly and simply from the heart of a passion,
for Tennyson does not quite sing, even so much as
Browning can; or one may be in quest of a "message"
and complain with Carlyle of Tennyson's lollipops—
yet lollipops are a relief to the strain and tedium of
sermons—but no candid critic, possessing ear and
imagination, can overlook the amazing extension of
the sensuous range of English lyrical poetry which
Tennyson had achieved by 1842. Only Coleridge, if
he had realised the promise of 1798, could, one thinks,
have gone further. The question remains, did he in
his later work not alone add some fresh prosodic and
stylistic achievements to those already attained, but
did his poetry catch the tone passionate and thought-
ful of the greatest lyrical poetry from Sappho to Burns
and Shelley? To some extent he did, if never su-
premely. No song in the 1842 volume has the plangent
quality of "Tears, idle tears" from *The Princess*, for

perhaps no thought moved Tennyson so simply and intensely as "the passion of the past," the thought that:

> All things are taken from us, and become
> Portions and parcels of the dreadful past.

In *In Memoriam* also, a sequence of meditative lyrics whose simpler style and verse heightens the impression of sincere, poignant feeling, there are sections of great lyrical power and beauty. If the hero of *Maud* is a somewhat hysterical person and the varying cadences not all equally effective, there are three rememberable lyrics: "I have led her home, my love, my only friend," "Come into the garden, Maud," and "O that 'twere possible."

The troubled spirit, too, in which Tennyson encountered the religious and political trend of the age, the beginning of which he had hailed with high hopes, found expression in his latest poems in some plangent notes—*Vastness, Crossing the Bar.* The later dialect poems, too, and *Rizpah* are written in a similar sombre tone. But the most notable additions which he made to his earlier work are of much the same kind, surprising and delighting rather by the freshness and beauty of their technique than by any deep note of feeling—*The Revenge, The Daisy,* the lines *To Virgil, The Voyage of Maeldune.*

In speaking of the great romantics I found it necessary to recognise that the lyrical afflatus which is so potent in their work did not express itself in the form of song alone, or even of more elaborate ode, but in rhapsodical poems, in short trochaic lines, and even in measures more proper to spoken poetry as decasyllabic couplets (Shelley's *Epipsychidion*), Spenserians

(*Adonais*), blank verse (*The Prelude, Alastor*), and other forms. To rhapsody Tennyson was not disposed, for rhapsody is more akin to song, and pure song is not his field. But on the other hand there is no great interval between his meditative lyrics and such blank-verse monodies as *Oenone, Tithonus, Ulysses, Lucretius,* and Tennyson's exquisite diction and variously cadenced blank verse—which moved too slowly and precisely for effective narrative—is seen to its fullest advantage in these meditative poems. As in "Tears, idle tears" one hardly misses the rhyme—delightful as Tennyson's rhyme can be—so musical is the effect of varying rhythm and well-chosen vowel and consonant.

A great virtuoso, not lending to the lyric of Burns and Blake and Shelley any new note of passion or fresh strain of thought but enlarging its capacity for the expression sensuously and musically of subtle, at times exotic, moods of feeling, that is Tennyson; and Browning is not very different. Is anything in Beddoes more exotic than one of Browning's earliest lyrics in *Paracelsus?*

> Heap cassia, sandal-buds and stripes
>   Of labdanum, and aloe-balls,
> Smeared with dull nard an Indian wipes
>   From out her hair: such balsam falls
>   Down sea-side mountain pedestals,
> From tree-tops where tired winds are fain,
> Spent with the vast and howling main,
> To treasure half their island-gain.
>
> And strew faint sweetness from some old
>   Egyptian's fine worm-eaten shroud
> Which breaks to dust when once unrolled;
>   Or shredded perfume, like a cloud

> From closet long to quiet vowed,
> With mothed and dropping arras hung,
> Mouldering her lute and books among,
> As when a Queen, long dead, was young.

What does it all mean, and what does it matter what it means? If Tennyson's *Mariana* and *Lilian* and "A spirit haunts the year's last hours" suggests lollipops or crystallised fruits, Browning's song savours of caviare; and Browning's lyrics, with all their dramatic interest, and, for some readers, inspiring thought, are full of such rich and subtle sensuous effects:

> Yet there's the dye, in that rough mesh,
>   The sea has only just o'er-whispered!
> Live whelks, each lip's beard dripping fresh
>   As if they still the water's lisp heard
> Through foam the rock-weeds thresh.

> Enough to furnish Solomon
>   Such hangings for his cedar house,
> That, when gold-robed he took the throne
>   In that abyss of blue, the Spouse
> Might swear his presence shone

> Most like the centre-spike of gold
>   Which burns deep in the blue-bell's womb,
> What time, with ardours manifold,
>   The bee goes singing to her groom,
> Drunken and overbold.

But Browning's virtuosity has a wider range than Tennyson's dramatically and metrically if he is less curiously studious of perfection, and he has a more genuine lyrical note. The author of the *Cavalier Tunes* could sing as Burns and Scott sang if with a difference, and nothing in *Maud* rises so soaringly as:

I send my heart up to thee, all my heart
  In this my singing.
For the stars help me, and the sea bears part,
  The very night is clinging
Closer to Venice streets to leave one space
  Above me, whence thy face
May light my joyous heart to thee its dwelling-place.

For some of Browning's lyrics "exotic" is too dignified
a word. *Nationality in Drinks* and others are in the
nature of freaks, for some of his feats in rhyming are
not unlike what delights one in the *Ingoldsby Legends*.
But of Browning's more serious lyrics it is necessary
to speak a little fully, for his critics have spent so much
time over Browning's thought and his various themes,
that, except for Professor Saintsbury's appreciative
analysis of his prosody, too little attention has been
given to his art as such. And one may begin with his
first experiment, in what is almost a lyrical drama,
Pippa Passes, the story of the little silk-winder of Asolo
whose songs as she passes various houses on her one
day of holiday precipitate one, dramatic crisis after
another. These are Browning's first dramatic lyrics;
lyrics, that is, which are supposed to be sung not by
the poet in his own person—like those of Blake and
Burns and Shelley and Keats and Wordsworth—but
by an imagined character, and not only that but a song
which implies a story. In this case the story is told,
not implied, and in *James Lee's Wife* and *In a Gondola*
the setting is elaborated, though not into so complete
a story as that of *Pippa*. But in almost all Browning's
songs a story is implied and, as in *Pippa* also, a great
deal is made of the setting, the scenery. Consider
*Cristina, A Lover's Quarrel, A Pretty Woman, Time's
Revenges, A Light Woman, The Last Ride Together,*

By the Fireside, Le Byron de nos Jours, Too Late, Youth and Art, Any Wife to Any Husband; and, to go outside the love songs, *Cavalier Tunes, The Heretic's Tragedy, The Lost Leader, How They Brought the Good News from Ghent to Aix*—round each you might build up a novel, or must recall a chapter in history (*The Heretic's Tragedy*), or imagine a piece of fictitious history (*How They Brought the Good News*).

But another thing is obvious if one goes back to *Pippa Passes,* and that is the very fanciful character of the story told or suggested. Of *Pippa Passes* a severe critic of Browning writes: "It is entirely free from certain defects which characterise his other pieces of a dramatic character. There is nowhere any violation of that natural probability which should govern the actions and emotions of the characters. . . . We know from our own observation, . . . that a remark overheard, a chance word spoken with not the least thought on the part of the speaker of affecting the course of another, often influences profoundly the whole life of the hearer. . . . The scheme of the poem . . . is worked out with consummate skill. It is both high morality and high art." That is true in a measure, yet I would add, as a qualification rather than a contradiction, a somewhat sentimental morality and a somewhat fanciful, even fantastic, if beautiful art. That Pippa's songs should by the operation of coincidence produce the beneficial effects they do is no more surprising or unnatural than are the abundant maleficent coincidences in Thomas Hardy's novels. What is surprising is that a girl of the kind described should sing such very Browningesque songs, and that these songs should produce the effect they do, especially the very enigmatical song which apparently sends Luigi

off to murder Metternich or the Kaiser in Vienna. I
dwell on this, not to depreciate the delightful poetry
of the little drama, but because I wish, starting from
Pippa Passes, to indicate what seem to me the recurrent
features of Browning's strange, exotic, bizarre, often
powerful lyrics. Many of them have not only a
dramatic but a picturesque setting, and a great part
of the sensuous charm of the songs comes from the
interwoven descriptions of that setting—the hot
Italian night in *A Serenade at the Villa:*

> Earth turned in her sleep with pain,
>   Sultrily suspired for proof:
> In at heaven and out again
>   Lightning! where it broke the roof,
> Bloodlike, some few drops of rain;

the scenery of the coast of France in *James Lee's Wife:*

> Oh, good gigantic smile o' the brown old earth,
>   This autumn morn! How he sets his bones
> To bask i' the sun, and thrusts out knees and feet
> For the ripple to run over in its mirth;
> Listening the while, where on the heap of stones
> The white breast of the sea-lark twitters sweet;

the solitary house in *A Lover's Quarrel:*

> Dearest! three months ago!
> Where we lived blocked-up with snow,—
>   When the wind would edge
>   In and in his wedge,
> In, as far as the point could go,—
>   Not to our ingle, though,
> Where we loved each the other so!

or again the Italian glen and the chapel in *By the
Fireside:*

> The chapel and bridge are of stone alike,
>   Blackish gray and mostly wet;
> Cut hemp-stalks steep in the narrow dyke.
>   See here again, how the lichens fret
> And the roots of the ivy strike!

the streets of Paris in *Respectability:*

> Ere we dared wander, nights like this,
> Thro' wind and rain, and watch the Seine,
> And feel the Boulevart break again
> To warmth and light and bliss.

The story suggested, the scenic setting so vividly presented are often fanciful in the highest degree, but just because they are only suggested—what *is* the story behind *The Laboratory* or *Too Late* or *Dis Aliter Visum?*—the poet does not get involved in the dramatic and sentimental difficulties which he encountered when, as in *The Blot in the 'Scutcheon,* he attempted to complete and make explicit the latent or just-outlined drama.

And the thought, the style, and the verse are of the same dramatic and also fanciful character. That Browning was a careless, awkward writer, who, as Jowett chirpingly declared, "has no form, or has it only by accident when the subject is limited. His thought and feeling and knowledge are generally out of all proportion to his powers of expression," that one can hardly credit, recalling the range of his metrical experiments and triumphs. Indeed, though there are elements in Browning's form which I dislike, the colloquial clichés in his blank verse, yet it seems to me almost the opposite of the truth. The thought is often simple enough, the feeling not a little sentimental. It is the cunning and surprising art, the picturesque touches, the subtle turn of fancy, the verse that carry it off. *Count Gismond* might have been written by Mrs. Hemans, as far as story and sentiment are concerned, in the style of *Casabianca*, or by Mrs. Browning in the manner of *Lady Geraldine's Courtship*, but neither could have rivalled Browning's art, his abrupt opening, the strange, picturesque, fanciful, and dramatic touches:

> And come out on the morning-troop
>   Of merry friends who kissed my cheek,
> And called me queen, and made me stoop
>   Under the canopy—(a streak
> That pierced it, of the outside sun,
> Powdered with gold its gloom's soft dun),

or, at the close:

> Over my head his arm he flung
>   Against the world; and scarce I felt
> His sword (that dripped by me and swung)
>   A little shifted in its belt:
> For he began to say the while
> How South our home lay many a mile.

There is hardly one of his love-lyrics that one cannot imagine being developed in another way, for the sentiment is generally quite simple when one catches it; but instead of gaining thereby, the poem would have lost what has kept it alive—Browning's subtle art, dramatic, fanciful, sensuous. He is as great a virtuoso, an artist delighting in experiments, as Tennyson, but with a different end in view. Tennyson is intent upon a single intense mood of feeling and its decorative and richly musical elaboration:

> "mouthing out his hollow oes and aes,
> Deep-chested music."

Browning is more dramatic and fanciful, liking the suggestion of a story, a psychological moment, eager to give to his style the actualities of colloquial speech even while he too decorates, and eager also to suggest how the mind works under the influence of feeling. This is where Browning's poems resemble Donne's— this rapid flow of thought; and they were both found obscure—"Donne himself for not being understood would perish" was the comment of Ben Jonson, who thought Donne "the first poet in the world in some things"—and partly but not entirely they were obscure for the same reason. They were, neither of them, averse to being a little enigmatic, to playing with learning familiar to themselves but which they must have known would not be familiar to their readers. Donne wrote a whole poem to show that he could be more obscure than Lord Herbert of Cherbury. Poets write to please themselves, and there is no good scolding them as though they were writers of advertisements; enigmatical poets have sometimes outlived their more popular rivals. In his later poems especially—*Pacchiarotto, Jocoseria* (confining myself to the lyrics)—Browning was, I think, at times quite intentionally enigmatic partly out of mischief, but also to hide as well as utter his feelings. His mind was moving restlessly over memories of his wife, perhaps his feeling for other women, and the problems of God and death and immortality, and he was not too anxious to be understood even by the Browning Society. But in his earlier, more dramatic lyrics there is a less deliberate source of difficulty, the rapidity and often fanciful character of his thought, with the further fact that Browning is probably the first poet of the subconscious or the threshold of the conscious and the subconscious. It is quite clear that the thoughts he puts into the mouths of Pippa and other characters are often such as would never have risen into their minds quite consciously. Browning is their interpreter. He had not, indeed, been taught by modern psychologists the importance of "the flow of consciousness"; he did not think that a poet will express himself best by saying nothing but may trust to the associations of his words and the images, allusions, and rhythms. No; Browning's idea is a rather different one. It is that our subconsciousness reasons more rapidly and subtly than our waking thoughts, which is not unlike Pascal's doctrine of the relation of intuition (finesse) to more explicit reasoning such as mathematics exemplify. In fact the inner consciousness of the speaker in *The Last Ride Together* or *James Lee's Wife* or *A Lover's Quarrel,* or of the lover in *A Serenade at the Villa,* or of the lady as the lover wishes or suspects it may be—still more of the speakers in some of the long monologues, *Mr. Sludge, "the Medium"* or *Bishop Blougram,* Don Juan in *Fifine at the Fair*—becomes the consciousness, the thought of Robert Browning, subtle, swift, fanciful, bizarre, a little enigmatical.

And what a wealth of lyrical poetry is contained in his work from *Paracelsus* to *Jocoseria* with:

> Never the time and the place
> And the loved one all together,

and *Ferishtah's Fancies* with its poignant *Epilogue:*

Oh Love—no, Love! All the noise below, Love,
  Groanings all and moanings—none of Life I lose!
All of Life's a cry just of weariness and woe, Love—
  "Hear at least, thou happy one!" "How can I, Love, but choose?"

.   .   .   .

Then the cloud-rift broadens, spanning earth that's under,
   Wide our world displays its worth, man's strife and strife's success:
All the good and beauty, wonder crowning wonder,
   Till my heart and soul applaud perfection, nothing less.

Only at heart's utmost joy and triumph, terror
   Sudden turns the blood to ice: a chill wind disencharms
All the late enchantment! What if all be error—
   If the halo irised round my head were, Love, thine arms?

Browning's philosophy, his ardent optimism, his "Christianity without tears," and his sentiment are a little out of fashion just now when our poets seem divided between the pessimism of Thomas Hardy and the Christianity, at once rollicking and menacing, of Chesterton. Even his love-poetry, the most varied in its treatment of the theme since John Donne, is a little suspected of Victorian sentimentalism, though the poet of the first episode in *Pippa Passes*, of *Respectability*, of *Too Late*, and of *Fifine at the Fair*, is not so squeamish as has been asserted. But if Browning as a great and solemn thinker has gone out with the Browning Societies, at any rate we can judge better than those of his day, whether early detractors or later admirers, of the amazing range of Browning's art, not least as a lyric poet. What a virtuoso he is, whether we consider the variety of his settings dramatic and fanciful, the sensuous richness of the descriptive element or its dramatic vividness, the Shakespearean originality and felicity of the imagery. Let me quote just one instance, from *Abt Vogler* dilating on his music:

And another would mount and march, like the excellent minion he
    was,
   Ay, another and yet another, one crowd but with many a crest,
Raising my rampired walls of gold as transparent as glass,
   Eager to do and die, yield each his place to the rest:

For higher still and higher (as a runner tips with fire,
    When a great illumination surprises a festal night—
Outlining round and round Rome's dome from space to spire)
    Up, the pinnacled glory reached, and the pride of my soul was in
        sight.

Recall, last but not least, the variety and felicity of his
metrical experiments and achievements. Sentimental
at times, fanciful often even to freakishness, Browning
may be, but no one today will with Jowett speak of
this great artist as an honest fellow "very generous
and truthful, quite incapable of correcting his literary
faults, which at first sprang from carelessness and an
uncritical habit and now are born and bred in him."
If Tennyson's lyrical and idyllic poetry recalls an
English garden of tree-shaded lawns and beds of tulips
and lilies and roses and chrysanthemums, Browning's
is a whole botanical garden full of exotics of different
centuries and different lands—*Cleon, Saul, A Heretic's
Tragedy, The Grammarian's Funeral, Holy-Cross Day,
A Tocatta of Galuppi's, Abt Vogler, On the Privilege
of Burial, Porphyria's Lover, The Pied Piper*, the
Epilogue in *Dramatis Personae* with the varied cadence
of the three speakers: the exultant rhythm of the first:

> On the first of the Feast of Feasts,
>   The Dedication Day,
> When the Levites join'd the Priests,
>   At the Altar in robed array,
> Gave signal to sound and say,—

How characteristic that line added to the ballad
verse. But the culminating verse adds yet another
that, as it were, completes what has seemed in the first
three an interrupted movement:

> Then the Temple filled with a cloud,
>   Even the House of the Lord;
> Porch bent and pillar bow'd:
>   For the presence of the Lord,
>   In the glory of His cloud,
> Had fill'd the House of the Lord.

As exultant as are the opening cadences so sombre is that which follows:

> Gone now! all gone across the dark so far,
>   Sharpening fast, shuddering ever, shutting still,
> Dwindling into the distance dies that star
>   Which came, stood, opened once!

Confidence but not exultation returns in the closing triads:

> Why, where's the need of Temple, when the walls
> O' the world are that? What use of swells and falls
> From Levites' choirs, Priests' cries, and trumpet-calls?
>
> That one Face, far from vanish, rather grows,
> Or decomposes but to recompose,
> Become my universe that feels and knows.

Arraigned as an artist, whether by Professor Jowett or Professor Raleigh, Browning might come into Court with that triad of lyrics—and there are others as good—as confidently as Sophocles with the Coloneus chorus.

A new movement or fashion in poetry is sure to call into being numbers of what I have called "mocking-birds"—poets of greater or less talent who catch up and render with a skill that may for a moment deceive even the elect, the note, the sentiment, and the manner of the more authentic voices. It would be harsh to give the name of "mocking-birds" to such poets as Elizabeth Barrett Browning, Alexander Smith, Sidney Dobell, who caught the ear of their own generation, and for a time, if the last two only for a very short time, were hailed as authentic poets by readers who had not yet discovered the author of *Bells and Pomegranates*. No poets could better illustrate the dangers that beset the romantic movement, especially as the first lyrical impulse and the cult of simplicity gave way to a deeper strain of sentimentality and a more conscious and elaborate virtuosity. Mrs. Hemans and James Montgomery and other earlier favourites—even Moore in his songs—nor would he himself have taken seriously his glittering Oriental tales—were comparatively simple souls, legitimate minor poets, piping of themes sentimental and romantic. But the "Spasmodics" took themselves very seriously indeed and endeavoured to write in a passionate and tragic manner, and in a highly imaginative phraseology learned, not from Scott and Byron, so much as from Shelley and Keats. And if one wishes to see what can be said for the eighteenth-century manner in lyrical poetry, of Akenside and his followers, I would suggest that one should read the short poem I have quoted from Cowper at p. 30, or the same poet's *Castaway*, and set it beside Mrs. Browning's *Sonnets from the Portuguese* or, to bring them still closer, her own *Cowper's Grave*. Cowper is expressing an anguish that transcends our normal conception, yet his language is simple, restrained, polite:

> Your sea of troubles you have pass'd
> And found the peaceful shore;
> I, tempest-toss'd and wreck'd at last,
> Come home to port no more.

Mrs. Browning has been kissed for the first time and she writes:

> First time he kiss'd me, he but only kiss'd
> The fingers of this hand wherewith I write;
> And ever since it grew more clear and white,
> Slow to world-greetings, quick with its "Oh list"
> When the angels speak, etc.

Well, lovers have always been allowed to speak in hyperboles, and one could parallel these extravagances from the seventeenth century, but the hyperboles would be more intellectual, less sentimental—to put it frankly, less forced and false. What real significance had angels for the author? There are, of course, better sonnets than this. I do not deny that Mrs. Browning was a poet, an artist, despite her careless rhymes and vague phrasing, of a considerable range of virtuosity. But her poetry abounds in vague thought, over-strained sentiment, and extravagant imagery. All the Spasmodics delight in these extravagant figures, and it was this that created the momentary glamour which their work produced—this and the fact that their sentiment was at the same time familiar and easy of appeal. One could gather from their works—and admirers *have* gathered—abundance of striking images and hyperboles. But Mrs. Browning was the best of this mid-century group, and besides the best of the sonnets has written some lyrics of real beauty. One, at any rate, is almost perfect. In

> What was he doing, the great God Pan,
> Down in the reeds by the river?

she has given to a thought of real import a fresh and felicitous treatment, in verse that flows with almost Shelleyan ecstasy and music. Her *Bianca among the*

Nightingales has some stanzas in which Italian passion
and scenery are blended:

> The Cypress stood up like a church
>   That night we felt our love would hold,
> And saintly moonlight seemed to search
>   And wash the whole world clean as gold;
> The olives crystallized the vales'
>   Broad slopes until the hills grew strong:
> The fire-flies and the nightingales
>   Throbbed each to either, flame and song.
> The nightingales, the nightingales.

But it is full of flaws, some of them—for it is a late
lyric—due to a desire to catch a little of her husband's
dramatic force:

> She lied and stole,
> And spat into my love's pure pyx
> The rank saliva of her soul.
> And still they sing, the nightingales,

which is distressing. Some of her simpler ballads and
lyrics too are not without charm, as *The Romance of
the Swan, Wine of Cyprus,* perhaps *The Deserted Garden,* but all suffer from her habit of careless, even painful, rhymes. *The Song of the Shirt* stands, with Hood's
Take Her up Tenderly, in a small class of lyrics with a
justifiable oratorical quality.

Of the work of other poets of the group, Sidney
Dobell's dreamy ballad *Keith of Ravelston* has established itself securely in every anthology of English
lyrics. Alexander Smith's *Glasgow* seems to me just to
fall short of the first class. In fact the lyrics of all
three of these poets—poets of no small virtuosity but
all alike prone to aim too high, to affect the manner of
poets of greater imaginative power than they themselves

possessed—are surpassed by one or two of the lyrics of a poet who had none of their virtuosity. Emily Brontë's lyric art was, as Sir Edmund Gosse pointed out long ago, very much that of Mrs. Hemans and L. E. L., but "Often rebuked, yet always back returning," "Cold in the earth—and the deep snow piled above thee," "Riches I hold in light esteem," and the great confession:

> No coward soul is mine,
> No trembler in the world's storm-troubled sphere:
> I see Heaven's glories shine,
> And faith shines equal, arming me from fear—

these are worth many *Sonnets from the Portuguese*. The Spasmodics used the language of passion; Emily Brontë had passion and thought, a vision of her own, though much of the verse printed since her death was the amusement of young dreamers inspired by Scott. Her metres are few and comparatively simple.

Fortunately for the development of English poetry, lyrical and other, Mrs. Browning and Sidney Dobell and Alexander Smith were not the only poets of the middle decades of the century—besides the two greater poets of whom I have spoken. Mrs. Browning's *Poems* and *Poems by C., E., and A. Bell* were both issued in 1846. In 1848 appeared Matthew Arnold's *The Strayed Reveller and other Poems* and *The Bothie of Tobernavuolich* by Arnold's friend and fellow-Rugbeian, Arthur Hugh Clough. The year 1850 witnessed a very remarkable series of publications. Wordsworth died and *The Prelude* was printed for the first time in full, a work that carries us back to the very beginnings of the great revolution in poetry, for the opening lines were composed as early as 1795—before the *Lyrical Ballads* had been planned or conceived—though it was not till the year of their publication that the great poem which was "to give pictures of Nature, Man, and Society" was fairly launched. In 1850 also appeared T. L. Beddoes' poetical drama *Death's Jest-Book*, a work planned in 1825 and so also a *revenant* from earlier times, a product of the aftermath of the first romantic movement, before the torch had passed to Tennyson and Browning. But the latter poets were still in their full strength and each published this year a remarkable work, *In Memoriam* and *Christmas Eve and Easter Day*, significant poems both, for the history of their own thought and feeling about life and death and the Christian faith to which each in his own way held firm while revealing in these poems their consciousness of the strength of the drift which was carrying the age away from the faith that alone gave confidence and hope to their minds. To the same year finally belong Mrs. Browning's *Sonnets from the Portuguese*, Dobell's *The Roman* (which with Alexander Smith's *A Life Drama* (1853) belongs to the Spasmodic eddy which I have touched on and which ultimately led nowhere) and, more important, *The Germ* of Dante Gabriel Rossetti and his friends, which was to prove the germ of a movement of no small significance alike for poetry and for art. Arnold's first volume was followed up in 1852, 1853, and 1855, his full poetic period closing with *Merope* in 1858, in which year appeared also William Morris's *Defence of Guenevere*. Rossetti's *Early Italian Poets* was issued in 1861; and most of his own earlier poems had been composed, and several of them printed, by 1862, though they were not all collected and published till 1870. I might just add to this dry but significant list Coventry Patmore's *Angel in the House* (1854-63), Fitzgerald's *Omar*

Khayyám (1859), Barnes's *Hwomely Rhymes* (1859), Swinburne's *The Queen Mother and Rosamund* (1861), and (in 1862) George Meredith's *Poems and Ballads* and Christina Rossetti's *Goblin Market and other Poems*. This will suffice to indicate the manner in which, as the century rounded the middle year, new poets were coming into evidence, how closely chariot pressed upon chariot as they approached and passed the pillar at the middle of the course, though the race may appear more exciting to us who look back than to readers of the day. But this is not all. As in the years between 1789 and 1798, new influences were in the air, new currents of thought were agitating the mind of England and Europe. Influences will not make poetry, but if the poets are there to receive them with other men, but on more sensitive plates, they will leave their record in many and complex ways, especially if these influences are of a metaphysical character. Political events count for less except in so far as they seem to give, or to promise to give, to ideas actuality. It was not the events of the French Revolution which gave us *The Prelude,* but the high hopes they excited in minds which had felt the influence of Rousseau's gospel and the disappointments that ensued.

What the new forces at work were will be clear if we recall certain other publications of these years. They were not primarily political, though 1848 was a stirring year. They concerned less men's political than their religious outlook, for the early years of Queen Victoria's reign had witnessed a great recovery of religious and Christian feeling under the influence of the Evangelical movement and, modifying this influence, the development of a more liberal Christianity. And now the ebb was beginning:

> The Sea of Faith
> Was once, too, at the full, and round earth's shore
> Lay like the folds of a bright girdle furl'd;
> But now I only hear
> Its melancholy, long, withdrawing roar,
> Retreating to the breath
> Of the night-wind down the vast edges drear
> And naked shingles of the world.

Chambers' *Vestiges of Creation* (1844), an anticipation of Darwin's *Origin of Species* (1859), had agitated Tennyson's sensitive soul and evoked some of the most plangent strains of *In Memoriam*. Strauss's *Das Leben Jesu* (translated by George Eliot, 1846), followed in 1842 by the work of Baur and the Tübingen School, was the chief cause of Browning's restatement of his own religious feeling in *Christmas Eve and Easter Day*. A wave of materialism, or to avoid misleading implications, of Lucretianism, which was to attain to its full height in the scientific writings that followed on the publication of Darwin's work, *e.g.* Huxley on *Man's Place in Nature* (1863) and Tyndall's famous address at Belfast, was rising and gathering strength. But at the same time another and counter-influence was rising also. The century was not done with the Middle Ages. The mediaevalism of the early Romantic Revival had not in this country rehabilitated the Catholic Church. From the Wartons to Sir Walter Scott the romantics had remained, when not sceptics, firm in the conviction that the Bible Protestantism of the Reformation was pure Christianity and that the Church of Rome, if not actually Antichrist, was "a mean and depraving institution," that the designs of her defenders in the sixteenth century "would have riveted on Scotland" (and England) "the chains of

antiquated superstition and spiritual tyranny." But
Scott had influenced, if Newman be right, those who
were beginning to think otherwise. The frost of
Protestant prejudice was relaxing. The growth of
"liberalism" was beginning to alarm those for whom
the authority of the Church had still a meaning, and
who, even before the new criticism of the Bible had
begun to undermine the foundation of historical
Protestantism, felt that, without the sanction of such
authority, their faith was in danger. Hurrell Froude's
Remains appeared in 1838 and the *Tracts for the Times*
began in 1841. As early as 1825 the magic of the
Middle Ages had made a Catholic of the young Cam-
bridge author of *The Broadstone of Honour* (1822, -23,
-26) and *Mores Catholici* (1831-42). Now within the
Church of England itself began a Catholic awakening
which has produced many results besides those which
concern my theme. For not all of those who felt
the charm of the Middle Ages, and studied them more
deeply than the earlier Romantics had done, were
drawn to Rome or even remained definitely Christian
—Ruskin, the Carlyle of *Past and Present*, Dante
Gabriel Rossetti, William Morris; nor was Catholicism
the only aspect of mediaeval literature which attracted
and delighted them. The chivalrous and the supernatural in ballad and romance made appeal to this as
to an earlier generation, to Rossetti and to Morris as
to Coleridge and Scott; and Rossetti and Morris and
Swinburne were to discover and revive that rival in
the Middle Ages of Christian devotion, the devotion
to woman, the cult not of the Virgin but of Lilith,
and to bring back into love-poetry an intensity of
devotion, sensuous and spiritual, which it had not
known since Shakespeare and Donne, if it was ever

quite acclimatised in England. It is rather to Dante and the Italians that this English poet of Italian blood goes back.

These were the two main currents that were flowing, carrying men away from their moorings, Protestant and Christian, in ways that distressed and agitated the older poets Tennyson and Browning—on the one hand the appeal or the repulsion excited by an ever-widening emancipation from accepted beliefs, the on-ward sweep of material science, and on the other the appeal of authority, a new view of the ages of faith and devotion if also of other things, the call of the great tradition of mediaeval faith and worship and art and poetry. The subject of the next two lectures will be the influence of these forces on the thought and feeling, and also on the art, the virtuosity, of the later poets of the century.

V

ARNOLD AND THE PRE-RAPHAELITE GROUP

THE stress which Matthew Arnold laid upon what he called "the classical school in poetry" need not blind us to the fact that the spirit of his own poetry is romantic through and through. In his survey, Byron and Wordsworth were the great forces in the romantic movement, and the tone of his own elegiac poetry is in truth more Byronic than Wordsworthian. Arnold's melancholy is a melancholy "compounded of many simples," of which the Byronic strain deepened by the continental inheritors of Byron's discontent is the chief element. What he was in revolt against was not really

the poetry of the greater romantics but the decorative
virtuosity in which that poetry seemed to be ending
in Tennyson, the fanciful, freakish strain in Browning
(whose intellectual vigour he respected), and the in-
sular, sentimental note of their philosophy of life.
What he opposed to this in his criticism as "the
classical school in poetry" was not what Byron had
preferred to his own poetry and that of his contemporaries, the poetry of Dryden and Pope, of Boileau
and Racine, for with these writers, English or French,
Arnold had no sympathy. It was the ancients, Latin
but especially Greek, and those modern poets who,
like Goethe in *Iphigenie auf Tauris* and some of his
rhymeless lyrics, had set themselves deliberately to
reproduce the form and spirit of Greek poetry. To
this we owe his Greek tragedy, *Merope,* and the less
regular *Empedocles on Etna;* his rhymeless irregular
lyrical poems, *The Strayed Reveller, The Youth of Nature, The Youth of Man, The Future, Rugby Chapel,
Heine's Grave, Haworth Churchyard.* To the same
effort after classical form we are indebted for those
fragments of epic, *Sohrab and Rustum,* and *Balder
Dead.* But what does it all come to? *Merope* is a failure.
Sohrab and Rustum and *Balder* are fine poems, but the
"fragment of an epic" is one of the varieties of nineteenth-century virtuosity. There is a touch of artifice
about them which is *not* classical. Of the irregular
lyrics those which admit rhyme are the more delightful
—*Resignation, Memorial Verses, A Summer Night,
The Buried Life, Dover Beach.* No; Arnold's debt to
the ancients is not these artificial experiments after the
manner of Goethe. It is a twofold one of sentiment
and of form. He owes to them an element in his
melancholy which distinguishes it from that of Byron

or the continental poets of discontent, Heine, Chateau-
briand, Lamartine—the note of resignation. It is not
Wordsworth's note, which is joy sustained by faith.
Arnold's appeal to nature for consolation or support
is at the opposite pole from Wordsworth's, as is his
whole conception of nature. Compare the consolatory
close to the story of Margaret with the closing stanzas
of *Obermann Once More*. The last word in the older
poet's speech is faith; Arnold's poem is an elegy on
the final departure of the faith which had sustained
and consoled men for centuries:

> While we believed, on earth he went,
> And open stood his grave.
> Men call'd from chamber, church, and tent;
> And Christ was by to save.
>
> Now he is dead! Far hence he lies
> In the lorn Syrian town;
> And on his grave, with shining eyes,
> The Syrian stars look down.

Nevertheless nature is still beautiful. Unaffected by
our sorrows or our illusions, she renews herself from
day to day and year to year in beauty and majesty:

> I awoke
> As out of sleep, and no
> Voice moved;—only the torrent broke
> The silence, far below.
>
> Soft darkness on the turf did lie.
> Solemn, o'er hut and wood,
> In the yet star-sown nightly sky,
> The peak of Jaman stood.
>
> Still in my soul the voice I heard
> Of Obermann!—away
> I turned; by some vague impulse stirr'd,
> Along the rocks of Naye

Past Sonchaud's piny flanks I gaze
And the blanch'd summit bare
Of Malatrait, to where in haze
The Valais opens fair,

And the domed Velan, with his snows,
Behind the upcrowding hills,
Doth all the heavenly opening close
Which the Rhone's murmur fills;

And glorious there, without a sound,
Across the glimmering lake,
High in the Valais-depth profound,
I saw the morning break.

Not from Wordsworth but from the Greeks, Homer, and the tragedians, especially Sophocles, Arnold derived the note of resignation which intensifies rather than relieves the melancholy of his poems, for the Greeks, if they believed in the gods, knew better than to think too well of them, or to imagine that the happiness of men was their chief concern. What the myths and experience had taught the Greeks—if Plato, anticipating Christianity, had protested—modern science, it seemed to Arnold, was teaching us: the powers that be are not primarily concerned with our happiness, with our deserts. But there are consolations, at least anodynes, for man born into a world where everything bears the mark of suffering:

Yet, Fausta, the mute turf we tread,
The solemn hills around us spread,
This stream that falls incessantly,
The strange-scrawl'd rocks, the lonely sky,
If I might lend their life a voice,
Seem to bear rather than rejoice.

The first of these anodynes is beauty, the beauty of

nature; and the second is song; and the third and greatest is love:

> Only—but this is rare—
> When a belovèd hand is laid in ours,
> When, jaded with the rush and glare
> Of the interminable hours,
> Our eyes can in another's eyes read clear,
> When our world-deafen'd ear
> Is by the tones of a loved voice caress'd,—
> A bolt is shot back somewhere in our breast,
> And a lost pulse of feeling stirs again;
>
> .   .   .   .
>
> And there arrives a lull in the hot race
> Wherein he doth forever chase
> That flying and elusive shadow, rest.
> An air of coolness plays upon his face,
> And an unwonted calm pervades his breast,
> And then he thinks he knows
> The hills where his life rose,
> And the sea where it goes.

In Greek poetry, too, and in Wordsworth, Arnold found a model in his quest of a simpler, purer style than the overwrought virtuosity of the great Victorians —a simpler style but more weighted with thought. For Arnold's poems are more "metaphysical" than even Browning's, in whose best poems the central thought, if one can discover it, is of less interest than the dramatic, sensuous, and metrical subtleties with which it is developed. Arnold's poetry is essentially a poetry of thought; everything of which he sings is seen through a medium of reflection, "sicklied o'er with the pale cast of thought." The lover in *Switzerland* is a very self-conscious, self-analytic lover, content in the end to escape from Marguerite to Nature. And so Arnold does not exactly sing. The nearest to actual song of his lyrics are the beautiful lines *To Fausta:*

> Joy comes and goes: hope ebbs and flows
> Like the wave,

where he is following Shelley, a little awkwardly, and "Strew on her roses, roses." His tone in general is that of a meditative chant rather than of song, in metres which, though irregular, do not give such an impression of virtuosity as the elaborate cadences and vowel-music of Tennyson or the varied and sometimes freakish experiments of Browning. His lyrics might be classified as poems in ballad or other comparatively simple forms, lyrics in irregular measures with or without rhyme, and odes in stanzas. In *Obermann* and *Obermann Once More* he has used the ballad measure in two poems which in their fulness of thought, clearness of vision and plangency of rhythm, are, especially the latter, the most simply effective of his metaphysical lyrical poems:

> She heard it, the victorious West
> In crown and sword array'd!
> She felt the void which mined her breast,
> She shiver'd and obey'd.
>
> She veil'd her eagles, snapp'd her sword,
> And laid her sceptre down;
> Her stately purple she abhorr'd,
> And her imperial crown;
>
> She broke her flutes, she stopp'd her sports,
> Her artists could not please;
> She tore her books, she shut her courts,
> She fled her palaces;
>
> Lust of the eye and pride of life
> She left it all behind,
> And hurried, torn with inward strife,
> The wilderness to find.

Tears washed the trouble from her face!
She changed into a child!
'Mid weeds and wrecks she stood—a place
Of ruin—but she smil'd!

Oh, had I lived in that great day,
How had its glory new
Fill'd earth and heaven, and caught away
My ravish'd spirit too!

The *Stanzas from the Grande Chartreuse* in sixains is in the same poignant, plangent, self-revealing style. One catches glimpses of the overstrained, protestant, moral upbringing which had wrecked the faith of Clough and Arnold:

For rigorous teachers seized my youth,
And purged its faith, and trimm'd its fire,
Show'd me the high white star of Truth,
There bade me gaze, and there aspire;
Even now their whispers pierce the gloom:
What dost thou in this living tomb?

Forgive me, masters of the mind!
At whose behest I long ago
So much unlearnt, so much design'd!
I come not here to be your foe.
I seek these anchorites, not in ruth,
To curse and to deny your truth.

.   .   .   .

Wandering between two worlds, one dead,
The other powerless to be born,
With nowhere yet to rest my head,
Like these, on earth I wait forlorn.
Their faith, my tears, the world deride;
I come to shed them at their side.

That is the new Byronism, melancholy but resigned, diagnosing its own malady in the loss of that faith against which Byron had protested passionately and which Shelley had denounced as *l'infâme;* and in the same poem Arnold lets us divine how much these two poets—Byron's "bleeding heart" and Shelley's "lonely wail"—had appealed to him in earlier days. *The Sick King in Bokhara* is a ballad poem too, but in long measure, and other longer poems in lyrical but regular measures are the somewhat enigmatic but beautiful *The New Sirens, A Palinode,* with its hint of suppressions, of conflicts between the puritan and the poet in Arnold; *Resignation,* the first full statement of his philosophy of the enigma of incompleteness that besets human life and all things that are; the *Memorial Verses* on Byron, Goethe, and Wordsworth; and one might add the blank verse, but lyrical blank verse, of the last section of *The Church of Brou:*

> So sleep, for ever sleep, O Marble Pair!

Of the shorter lyrics some are in a didactic, gnomic vein—*Revolutions, Morality, Self-Dependence, Progress, The Last Word,* and others—which has lost interest. The best are those gathered, at one time or another, under the heading *Switzerland* and *Fugitive Leaves,* or on the same theme, love poems of one, like Shelley, conscious of the mutual impenetrability of human souls, conscious also of a heart divided between human love and the passion of contemplation:

> Far, far from each other
>   Our spirits have grown;
> And what heart knows another?
>   Ah! who knows his own?
>
> Blow, ye winds! lift me with you!
>   I come to the wild.
> Fold closely, O Nature!
>   Thine arms round thy child. . . .

> Ah, calm me! restore me!
>   And dry up my tears
> On thy high mountain-platforms,
>   Where morn first appears,
>
> Where the whites mists, for ever,
>   Are spread and upfurl'd;
> In the stir of the forces
>   Whence issued the world.

That is from *Parting,* and in the same vein are *Human Life* (which was never included in the series), and *Isolation,* the best known of Arnold's shorter lyrics.

A second class is composed of those meditative lyrics, rhymed or unrhymed, which were suggested less perhaps by the Greek choruses than by similar poems of Goethe and Heine. To this class belong the three lovely songs of Callicles in *Empedocles:*

> Far, far from here,
> The Adriatic breaks in a warm bay
> Among the green Illyrian hills;
>
> Oh, that Fate had let me see
> That triumph of the sweet persuasive lyre,
> That famous final victory,
> When jealous Pan with Marsyas did conspire!

and

> Not here, O Apollo!
> Are haunts meet for thee.
> But, where Helicon breaks down
> In cliffs to the sea.

But the earliest of these longer irregular lyrics was the delightful *The Forsaken Merman,* in which the varying measures are managed with a finer musical effect than Arnold always achieved. To these were added, in the volume of 1852, *The Youth of Nature, The Youth of*

Man, The Buried Life, The Future, which seems to me sometimes the best allegorical poem in the language, the only allegory in verse which does not give one a headache (as is, Dickens says, the way of allegory) but strikes home in every vivid, significant stanza; and last and greatest, *A Summer Night,* the most plangent and the noblest utterance of Arnold's melancholy and resignation, the resignation of a Marcus Aurelius:

> Plainness and clearness without shadow of stain!
> Clearness divine!
> Ye Heavens, whose pure dark regions have no sign
> Of languor, though so calm, and though so great,
> Are yet untroubled and unpassionate;
> Who, though so noble, share in the world's toil,
> And, though so task'd, keep free from dust and soil!
> I will not say that your mild deeps retain
> A tinge, it may be, of their silent pain
> Who have long'd deeply once, and long'd in vain:
> But I will rather say that you remain
> A world above man's head, to let him see
> How boundless might his soul's horizon be,
> How vast, yet of what clear transparency!
> How it were good to sink there, and breathe free.
> How fair a lot to fill
> Is left to each man still!

Of the additions made to these in later volumes— *Rugby Chapel, Heine's Grave, Dover Beach*—the greatest is the last with its vivid opening description, the felicitous allusion to Sophocles, and the passionate close.

These irregular lyrics are an experiment, but they do not give quite the same impression of virtuosity, of metrical experiments made for their own sake, experiments in music and mood, as some of Tennyson's and Browning's. They rather, like the choruses in

Milton's *Samson,* suggest a subordination of metrical effect to the claims of thought, an effort to secure a rhythm that echoes and emphasises the thought rather than adorns it. The thoughts stand out clear, even with a certain austerity; they do not "lie like bees in their own sweetness drown'd," as in *The Lotos-Eaters* or *The Vision of Sin.*

There remain Arnold's two odes in regular stanzaic form, *The Scholar Gipsy* and *Thyrsis,* poems whose metrical form and felicitous sensuous touches confess the poet's debt to Keats, but which in thought and feeling are a repetition of the ever-recurring Arnoldian melancholy and resignation, a poet's mood which, like Byron's, represented only one phase of his mind. The letters and prose-works show that he like Byron had quite other sides to his nature. Of the two *The Scholar Gipsy* is the happier and fresher in conception and as a whole the more perfect; but the flower stanzas in *Thyrsis,* and some of the other verses, fall in no way behind. If there are more poignant and plangent lyrics, these are the richest in sensuous and musical beauty.

Arnold's endeavour to bring poetry back to a greater simplicity of form while weighting it with thought met with very indirect support from the group of young poets who emerged between the publication of The *Germ* in 1850 and 1870. Rossetti, Morris, Swinburne, Christina Rossetti—they all in different ways felt the influence of the thought that was disintegrating the earlier Victorian tradition. But they were artists, not thinkers—with degrees of individual exception—and their work was to be a further elaboration and enrichment of the amazing virtuosity of English poetry in this century, especially lyrical poetry. In them a tendency of the romantic revival from the first imitation of the old ballads, and the spurious Middle English poems of Chatterton, attained to its most complete manifestation—the revival of old moods and old modes, the playing (as one might put it) at being a mediaeval poet of love and Catholic devotion, a Greek poet, lyrical or tragic. It is, of course, a sophisticated reproduction in which modern feeling is subtly blended with or disguised in an antique fashion. Of the prophetic strain in the poetry of the earlier romantics, Blake, Wordsworth, Shelley, or the didactic strain in Tennyson and Browning, there is nothing—or nothing really effective—in the poetry of the Pre-Raphaelites. Art was their religion. Of the elements that are combined in the complex effect of a poem—thought (what the poem states); the colour given by the words the poet uses and the syntax of his sentences; his imagery and the rhythm, the melody and harmony of his verse, the tendency of romantic poetry had been to lay more and more stress upon the last three—colour, imagery, harmony—at the expense of the first, which the eighteenth-century poets had always regarded as the core and justification of the whole. "Poetry," Johnson said, "is the art of uniting pleasure with truth, by calling imagination to the help of reason." *The Vanity of Human Wishes*, *The Deserted Village*, the *Ode on a Distant Prospect of Eton College* are all poems that make a definite statement which the poetry decorates and enforces. But the thought of even the prophetic poems of Blake or Wordsworth or Shelley is suggested rather than stated, is mystical, an attempt to define a mood which transcends clear thinking. And in the work of poets less burdened with a message to deliver, colour and imagery and music are the poet's chief interest whatever the ostensible purpose. The statement, if there be one, is only a contributor, it may be a small contributor, to the total impression. What does Coleridge state in *The Ancient Mariner*—except by way of concession to Wordsworth—or Keats in his odes, or Tennyson in *The Lady of Shalott* and *The Lotos-Eaters,* or even Browning in *A Heretic's Tragedy* or *Childe Roland to the Dark Tower Came?* But the poet who first, from his study of Keats and especially of Tennyson, as well as doubtless from the bent of his own genius, grasped clearly this tendency of romantic poetry, and with a conscious virtuosity set himself to push it a little further and subordinate statement to suggestion, colour and music, especially the last, was the American poet of the thirties and forties, Edgar Allan Poe, the poet of *The Raven* and *Ulalume* and *Annabel Lee* and *Annie* and *The Haunted Palace* and *To Helen;* "the artful, subtle, irresistible song of Poe, the new music which none that has heard it can forget," to quote Henley.

I have no thought of suggesting indebtedness to Poe, but the Pre-Raphaelite poets sought the same kind of effect, to communicate a mood less by definite statement—what statement there is being dramatic rather than personal—than by suggestion or symbolism, by imagery, and by subtle rhythms and patterns of sound. Of the three chief poets Rossetti relies most on suggestion, atmosphere. Morris's most constant appeal is to the eye. Even when it is night he sees as well as hears:

> but nought he saw
> Except the night-wind twitching the loose straw
> From half-unloaded keels, and nought he heard
> But the strange twittering of a caged *green* bird
> Within an Indian ship;

for Swinburne the music of his verse is all in all. "He has no eyes" and his statements are negligible, so that he was apparently genuinely surprised when the Victorians, taking him at his word, condemned *Poems and Ballads* as a direct incentive to vice. But there was an element of truth in the protest. Swinburne's dramatic lyrics were a challenge to the limitations which Evangelical morals had set to the poet and the artist, a definite refusal to accept the dogma that poetry must edify.

Dante Gabriel Rossetti's romantic inspiration came from German poetry. Like Scott earlier, he translated Bürger's *Lenore*—preserving more closely than Scott the form of the original—and it was the supernatural thrill which appealed to his imagination. Of three of his maturer poems in ballad form, *Sister Helen*, *Rose Mary*, and *The King's Tragedy*, this is the, or a principal, *motif*. But the influence of the German ballads was reinforced and modified by that of Italian *trecentisto* poetry and primitive Italian art, for Rossetti was artist as well as poet. It was from thence that, both as painter and poet, he learned the power of clear, pure pictures and of vivid detail to convey the suggestion of intense feeling, an all-absorbing mood. This was the essence of Pre-Raphaelitism. The psychological fact on which the effect depends is that we do, in moments of heightened feeling, observe even irrelevant details with a singular vividness. Rossetti's short lyric *The Woodspurge* is a simple illustration:

> From perfect grief there need not be
> Wisdom or even memory:
> One thing then learnt remains to me,—
> The woodspurge has a cup of three.

In two of the poems first printed, though later revised, *The Blessed Damozel* and *My Sister's Sleep*, Rossetti made use of the device in poems aiming at the two kinds of effect which the group especially cultivated, whether in poem or painting—the revival in a sophisticated way of a mediaeval mood and the realistic rendering of a quite modern scene and poignant experience. In the first, a poem that will always connect itself withRossetti's name as closely as *The Ancient Mariner* with that of Coleridge, written in a simple, six-line ballad measure, this use of vivid, realistic detail is strangely heightened by its combination with touches of Dantesque sublimity and pictorial decoration:

> Her robe, ungirt from clasp to hem
>   No wrought flower did adorn,
> But a white robe of Mary's gift,
>   For service meetly worn;
> The hair that lay along her back
>   *Was yellow like ripe corn.*
>
> .   .   .   .   .   .
>
> It was the rampart of God's house
>   That she was standing on;
> By God built over the sheer depth
>   The which is Space begun:
> *So high, that looking downward thence*
>   *She scarce could see the sun.*
>
> It lies in Heaven, across the flood
>   Of ether, as a bridge.
> Beneath, the tides of day and night
>   With flame and darkness ridge
> The void, as low as where *this earth*
>   *Spins like a fretful midge.*
>
> Around her, lovers newly met
>   'Mid deathless love's acclaims,
> Spoke ever more among themselves
>   Their heart-remembered names;

And the souls mounting up to God
Went by her like thin flames.

.   .   .   .

From the fixed place of Heaven she saw
Time like a pulse shake fierce
Through all the worlds.

In *My Sister's Sleep* the same kind of intense effect is secured by more homely but equally vivid details:

Without, there was a cold moon up,
    Of winter radiance sheer and thin;
    The hollow halo it was in
Was like an icy crystal cup.

Through the small room, with subtle sound
    Of flame, by vents the fireshine drove
    And reddened. In its dim alcove
The mirror shed a clearness round.

.   .   .   .

Our mother rose from where she sat:
    Her needles, as she laid them down,
    Met lightly, and her silken gown
Settled: no other noise than that.

I do not know that Rossetti wrote any poems that give more the effect of something new and surprising than these, except the two in which he revived the intense devotional mood of mediaeval Catholicism, *World's Worth* and *Ave*, both much elaborated in revisions, the latter at some cost. For over-elaboration was one effect of Rossetti's devotion to his art, and to my mind most of the ballads to which I have referred at the outset suffer from it; and so notably do the sonnets in *The House of Life*. For the supernatural and the devotional were not the only moods which Rossetti recaptured from Italian poetry and painting. In the sonnets of the first part of the above collection, and in a number of lyrical poems, whether elaborate like *The Stream's Secret* and *Love's Nocturn* (with its echoing rhymes) or simpler, if as heavily laden, *The Song of the Bower*, and

> A little while a little love
> The hour yet bears for thee and me,

and *Love-Lily* and *Insomnia*, as well as in ballads like *Troy Town* and *Eden Bower*, Rossetti revived the tense, single-minded passion, spiritual or sensuous or both, of Mediaeval and Renaissance love-poetry. In Rossetti the sensuous predominates, and there is, after all, a world of difference between Rossetti's sonnets and those of Dante or Petrarch or Shakespeare or the *Songs and Sonets* of John Donne. He is closer akin to Boccaccio and to Chaucer in his version of *Il Filostrato*. For the object of Rossetti's devotion is his wife, and there is no room in this strain of mutual love, heart pressed to heart, for the conflict and interchange of moods—adoration, eulogy, impatience, reproach—which agitate the older sequences. No conflict enters to sharpen the warm, heavy atmosphere of Rossetti's voluptuous passion till Death begins to loom upon the horizon, when the thought and imagery do grow clearer and more poignant:

> Cling heart to heart; nor of this hour demand
>   Whether in very truth, when we are dead,
> Our hearts shall wake to know Love's golden head
>   Sole sunshine of the imperishable land;
> Or but discern, through night's unfeatured scope,
> Scorn-fixed at length the illusive eyes of hope.

But perhaps the most arresting, the most purely Rossettian, are those in which statement yields place

to symbolism and passionate cry in the strange but
arresting sequence, *Willow-Wood*. In two poems, lastly,
the dramatic ballad *Dante at Verona* and the fine, chiming lyric, *The Burden of Nineveh*, Rossetti escapes
from the somewhat heavy atmosphere of his poems of
love and the supernatural, and catches a more masculine
tone of meditation. In the first, as in many of his poems,
the influence of Browning's dramatic manner is obvious,
but the clear, vivid imagery and the cadences are his
own:

> Arriving only to depart,
>   From court to court, from land to land,
>   *Like flame within the naked hand*
> *His body bore his burning heart,*
>   That still on Florence strove to bring
>   God's fire for a burnt offering.

Of the Pre-Raphaelite poets Morris alone was
almost claimed for the Anglican Church of the Oxford
Movement by his love of the Middle Ages and the
beauty of Gothic churches. That phase soon passed
and left no mark on his poetry or prose. It was the
Middle Ages as he *saw* them in architectural and pictorial remains and in the pictures conjured up in his
mind by Froissart and Malory and Chaucer that
fascinated him; and the spirit which he divined
behind and in these works was less the devotional—
once the charm of *Mores Catholici* had passed away—
than the passionate soul of great lovers and great
fighters and goodly builders and painters and crafts-
men. His early lyrics, or what survive of them in the
volume of 1858, *The Defence of Guenevere and Other
Poems*, have not the close, heavy atmosphere of Rossetti's, but the purpose of the poet is the same—the

rendering of an intense, passionate, unwavering mood. Malory and Froissart have equally enthralled him, the romantic, passionate dreams of the Middle Ages and the passionate, if brutal, realities which Froissart presents in such sharp contrast to the dreams. And for Morris both *were* dreams, vivid and sharp, into which he threw himself with the same passionate ardour with which Scott had lived in the world of the old ballads; but the ardour is more purely that of the artist, more that of Keats in *La Belle Dame sans Merci,* which was, he said later, the germ of all the poetry of his group. Scott's poems are a substitute for the life of action from which he was cut off; he divines through the ballads the men of whom they told, and they are genial, burly men such as he still meets. Morris lives more entirely in the picture and the dream, a world of bright colours and expressive gestures, and persons seen as in tapestries and frescoes, vivid but in two dimensions only; and he lives in imagination the life of fierce loves and hates which for him is the whole life of the Middle Ages he had loved from a boy and the Scandinavian heroes whom he came to love. Of the humour, the touches of good sense and philosophy, which give a more rounded reality to the world of Chaucer and Scott, there is nothing. So, to my mind, the best of Morris's poetry is lyrical, for in the intenser mood of which song is the expression one misses these other qualities less. In the long poems from *Jason,* through *The Earthly Paradise* to even *Sigurd the Volsung,* one is a little oppressed by the monotony of the mood, the one mood of love and longing and regret. He was never again quite so vivid, so intense, so dramatic as in *The Defence of Guenevere* and *Sir Peter Harpdon's End* (a parallel in its Pre-Raphaelitic realism to *My*

Sister's Sleep) and *Shameful Death* and *The Haystack in the Floods*; never made more telling use of passionate, expressive gesture:

> Her tired feet looked cold and thin,
>   Her lips were twitch'd, and wretched tears,
>   Some, as she lay, roll'd past her ears,
> Some fell from off her quivering chin.
>
> Her long throat stretch'd to its full length,
>   Rose up and fell right brokenly;
>   As though the unhappy heart were nigh
> Striving to break with all its strength.

Nor was he ever again quite so boyishly, so delightfully romantic as in some of the ballads with refrains—*Two Red Roses across the Moon* and *The Eve of Crécy* and *The Sailing of the Sword*—if the refrains lend themselves a little to Calverley's parody, "Butter and eggs and a pound of cheese."

But it will not quite do to say with the late Mr. Dixon Scott that the effect of these poems was a kind of accident, due to the vividness with which Morris saw and painted, that he had no cunning of word and rhythm, and that his later, more diffuse poetry is altogether of another kind. The hearty, cheerful Morris of whom the *Life* tells never found his way *into* the poetry, which is all in one key. The mood of the early poems is the mood of the later, if never again expressed with such dramatic intensity, in such sharp, vivid pictures. He wrote hereafter in a softer strain, in a more diffuse and equable style, in a more lulling verse, but the burden of it all is the same—delight in beauty, the beauty of nature and of craftsmanship, things made with human hands, the beauty of strength and courage, courage in the face of death which awaits all men, "that contemplation of inexhaustible melancholy whose shadow eclipses the brightness of the world," as Shelley said and Morris felt, while he felt also the splendour which it lends to the heroism, the intensity it gives to the love, of men and women. And love is the central fire of all Morris's poems, narrative and lyrical. If his love-poems have not the dramatic variety of Browning's, he is an even more ardent devotee, less sensuous than Rossetti, less ethereal and inhuman than Shelley. For Morris the mutual love of a man and a woman, passion and affection blended, is quite simply the greatest good the world has to give, and if the simplicity and monotony of his treatment becomes a little wearisome in the tales, it has inspired some of the loveliest lyrics in the language. For the quintessence of Morris's poetry is in the lyrics, those scattered through the tales, verse and prose, and those gathered together in the last delightful volume, *Poems by the Way* (1891). In *Jason* there is "I know a little garden close," and in *The Earthly Paradise* the beautiful songs of the months in Chaucer's "Troilus" stanza of which, though all are delightful in their rendering of English scenery, the gem, in passion and cadence (the drawing out of the sentence through the stanza), is *October*:

> O Love, turn from the unchanging sea and gaze
> Down these grey slopes upon the year grown old,
> A-dying 'mid the autumn-scented haze,
> That hangeth o'er the hollow in the wold,
> Where the wind-bitten ancient elms infold
> Grey church, long barn, orchard and red-roofed stead,
> Wrought in dead days for men a long while dead.

But some of the loveliest of Morris's lyrics are in the *Poems by the Way*, written when his love of love had made him a Socialist. Here is *Hope Dieth: Love Liveth*, *Of the Three Seekers*, the beautiful *Message of the March Winds*, *Iceland First Seen*, *Love Fulfilled*, and the surprising and entrancing *Meeting in Winter*:

> They shall open, and we shall see
> The long street litten scantily
> By the long stream of light before
> The guest-hall's half-open door;
> And our horses' bells shall cease
> As we reach the place of peace;
> Thou shalt tremble, as at last
> The worn threshold is o'er-past,
> And the firelight blindeth thee:
> Trembling shalt thou cling to me
> As the sleepy merchants stare
> At thy cold hands slim and fair,
> Thy soft eyes and happy lips
> Worth all lading of their ships.
>
> O my love, how sweet and sweet
> That first kissing of thy feet,
> When the fire is sunk alow,
> And the hall made empty now
> Groweth solemn, dim and vast!
> O my love, the night shall last
> Longer than men tell thereof,
> Laden with our lonely love!

Few poets have written so abundantly, unless it be Spenser, on so few notes, in so narrow a range of moods, and yet written perhaps nothing that is quite empty and nothing that any one but a poet could have written.

And then came Swinburne; his unnoticed *Queen Mother* and *Rosamond* (1860) following *The Defence of Guenevere* by four years, while between them and the appearance of the more decisive *Atalanta in Calydon*

(1865) and *Poems and Ballads* (1866), George Meredith, Christina Rossetti, and Coventry Patmore all made their *début*, but of them later. It is difficult for the present generation to realise the effect of Swinburne's lyrical ecstasies on readers of the seventies and eighties. *Poems and Ballads* was for lovers of poetry as great an event as the *Origin of Species* for biologists and theologians. It was not alone the new and resounding rhythms. As with Byron's poetry earlier, what shocked and outraged some critics was just what delighted younger readers, the splendid audacity with which the poet challenged conventions and asserted the right of poetry to express all the desires and joys and sorrows of the human spirit, the perennially recurring reaction of the nature of man against his self-imposed repressions. Mr. Nicolson's cool appreciation of *Poems and Ballads* and selection of *Songs Before Sunrise* as Swinburne's most characteristic and greatest work marks very clearly the change of sentiment, for there can be no doubt that it was the boldness and passion of the love-songs that delighted us—*Dolores* and *The Triumph of Time* and *Hesperia* and "Let us go hence, my songs; she will not hear," and "Kissing her hair, I sat against her feet," and in *Atalanta* the chorus:

> What had'st thou to do being born,
>   Mother, when winds were at ease,
> As a flower of the springtime of corn,
>   A flower of the foam of the seas?

and later in the second series of *Poems and Ballads* the ringing verses of *At a Month's End*—it was these and the boldly pagan strain of the other choruses in *Atalanta* and the *Garden of Proserpine* and the *Hymn to Proserpine:*

Thou hast conquered, O pale Galilean; the world has grown grey
    from thy breath;
We have drunken of things Lethaean, and fed on the fulness of death.

.   .   .   .   .   ,   .

Not as thine, not as thine was our mother, a blossom of flowering
    seas,
Clothed round with the world's desire as with raiment, and fair as
    the foam,
And fleeter than kindled fire, and a goddess, and mother of Rome.
For thine came pale and a maiden, and sister to sorrow; but ours,
Her deep hair heavily laden with odour and colour of flowers,
White rose of the rose-white water, a silver splendour, a flame,
Bent down unto us that besought her, and earth grew sweet with
    her name.
For thine came weeping, a slave among slaves, and rejected; but she
Came flushed from the full-flushed wave, and imperial, her foot on
    the sea.
And the wonderful waters knew her, the winds and the viewless ways,
And the roses grew rosier, and bluer the sea-blue stream of the bays.

—these were the strains that swept us off our feet, not necessarily from any deep sympathy with illicit passion or anti-Christian sentiment but because they provided so satisfying a *catharsis* for moods that will haunt the heart of youth. It may be that Swinburne's art had grown more cunning and perfect in the *Songs before Sunrise,* but these had two faults compared with *Atalanta* and *Poems and Ballads.* The passion was somewhat empty, for if Byron's conception of liberty was, so Lord Morley said, a purely negative one, Swinburne had no conception at all (and no people has grown more tired of mere liberty than the Italians), and in the second place the lyrical poems were growing too long. One needs the support of more thought to keep one's interest sustained through rhapsodies of such length as *Italy* and similar tirades. Even *Hertha,* which has been so much commended, says the

same thing over and over again. No; the poem which
has something of the old sting is the *Prelude*, where
Swinburne recants his early excesses and catches fire
from their recollection:

> Play then and sing; we too have played,
> We likewise, in that subtle shade.
>> We too have twisted through our hair
>> Such tendrils as the wild Loves wear,
> And heard what mirth the Maenads made,
>> Till the wind blew our garlands bare
> And left their roses disarrayed,
>> And smote the summer with strange air,
> And disengirdled and discrowned
> The limbs and locks that vine-wreaths bound,

and I cannot but think that to the end something of
the old "salt and savour" comes into Swinburne's
poetry when the theme is the old one of love—as in
some of the songs in the second *Poems and Ballads*
(1878), the already mentioned *At a Month's End* with
the fierce leap of the intermingled trochees and
iambs:

> As a star feels the sun and falters,
>> Touched to death by diviner eyes—
> As on the old gods' untended altars
>> The old fire of withered worship dies,
>
> .   .   .   .
>
> So once with fiery breath and flying
>> Your winged heart touched mine and went,
> And the swift spirits kissed, and sighing,
>> Sundered and smiled and were content,

and "I saw my soul at rest upon a day," "Could'st
thou not watch with me one hour?" "I hid my heart in
a nest of roses," "Now the days are all gone over," and

> Love laid his sleepless head
> On a thorny rosy bed,

and *Choriambics,* and

> For a day and a night Love stayed with us, played with us,
> Folded us round from the dark and the light;

and, even later, if *Tristram of Lyonesse* is not a successful narrative poem it is a splendid rhapsody, and the most Wagnerian piece of music in English poetry is surely *Iseult at Tintagel,* that unrelenting agony of passionate love communing with itself, each pause in the monologue punctuated by the merciless chorus of wind and sea:

> And all their past came wailing in the wind,
> And all their future thundered in the sea,

and then the cruel irony of the close:

> and he (*i.e.* Hodain, the hound)
> Laid his kind head along her bended knee,
> Till round his neck her arms went hard, and all
> The night passed from her as a chain might fall:
> But yet the heart within her, half undone,
> Wailed, and was loth to let her see the sun.
> And ere full day brought heaven and earth to flower,
> Far thence, a maiden in a marriage bower,
> That moment hard by Tristram, oversea,
> Woke with glad eyes Iseult of Brittany.

The *Adieux à Marie Stuart* of the same volume are touched with the same fire:

> Love hangs like light about your name
> As music round the shell:
> No heart can take of you a tame
> Farewell.

In disagreement from Mr. Nicolson I would maintain that Swinburne's poetry has fire as well as music only

when its theme is passion. On all other themes, even
liberty, even the sea, of which he sings, after all, from
the beach, even other poets, even children, there is
always a suggestion in the exalted, too-long-sustained
chants, of frothiness,

> Double, double
> toil and trouble.

For doubtless there was a certain amount of illusion
in the spell Swinburne cast over us. He was not a
great love-poet as Donne was, and Shakespeare, and
even William Morris. Of love he knows only one
mood. Of that no more than of any other theme does
he write as one who has seen

> The very pulse of the machine

and so is able to open our eyes to unrealised values.
It was the mode, not the mood, which bewitched
us. That was evident from the first in some poems
—the spring chorus in *Atalanta,* so delightful in its
movement yet as a real interpretation of the season
not comparable for a moment with Keats's *Autumn;*
Itylus with its miraculous suggestion of the piercing
song of the nightingale and the quick swish of the
darting swallow's wings; and many another where the
meaning, the feeling, count for next to nothing. The
final significance of Swinburne's poetry is that in it the
amazing virtuosity of the lyrical poetry of the century
attained a limit. He could reproduce and give new
musical values to any mode he chose—the Italian
canzone or *sestina,* mediaeval miracle, border ballad,
French rondels, Greek drama and ode and choral
song, Elizabethan verse, dramatic and lyrical—he

could revive them all, and invent new rhythms and stanzas at will, and still be himself, unmistakable. If he had only had a little more that was rememberable to say, given fresh worth to some aspect of our experience as all the greatest poets have done. There was after all something a little ominous in Swinburne's early passion for Landor.

Of lesser poets whom one, rightly or wrongly, connects with this movement, Christina Rossetti had the most spontaneous lyrical note. Her longest poems, *Goblin Market* and *The Prince's Progress,* ethical and allegorical in content, are lyrical in form, and it is in light-winged, essentially singing measures, with freely interchanging cadences—iambic, trochaic, anapaestic— rather than the more uniformly iambic ballad rhythm to which her brother and Morris leaned—that the most of her, generally short, pieces are composed, excepting the sonnets and some of the more solemn devotional pieces. The distinctively Pre-Raphaelitic strands, the exotic cultivation of older moods and modes, the vivid, picturesque presentation of emotionally significant details—these things are not obvious in her poetry. The feelings she expresses are simple and personal and not numerous—a love of breezy English scenery, fresh green meadows sprinkled with lambs, woods and orchards; love, a suppressed passion, sacrificed to duty and devotion, a feeling to which we owe some of the more poignant of her songs: "Now, did you mark a falcon," "As rivers seek the sea," "Love strong as death is dead," "I took my heart in my hand," "Come to me in the silence of the night," "I cannot tell you how it was," and "Somewhere or other there must surely be." Lastly there are the devotional poems, the poems of the devotion for which she sacrificed love. It cannot be said that they express a compensating ecstasy. The author of the weird and haunting "Sleep at Sea," "Does the road lead uphill all the way?" "Passing away, saith the world, passing away," "By day she woos me, soft exceeding fair," is strangely akin to Donne, whose religious poetry is also overshadowed by fear and breathes the spirit of one who would feel more love and confidence than he does. They are both far from the spirit of Herbert whose *The Temple* is a sonnet-sequence in which the lovers are God and his own soul, the longing of Vaughan to break through the dividing veil, the ecstasies of Crashaw. She had neither the passion and courage of Emily Brontë nor the fine ardent spirit and eager sympathy of the more faulty artist Elizabeth Barrett Browning. It is the lyrical spontaneity and the delicate, conscientious art of her cloistered poetry that has given it such life as it has.

Arthur O'Shaughnessy's *Music and Moonlight* (1874) has the qualities its name indicates, and illustrates in the clear way that minor work often does the subordination of content to suggestion by colour and harmony. He had, Professor Saintsbury declares, the "characteristic of Irish word musicians, since Moore at least—the air almost of an improvisation"; and "in this respect, as in some others, is more like Poe than any purely English poet." He is, one might say, a Moore of a later fashion in poetry, remembered by two poems in which there is, besides the light and cunning music of many others, that qualification to which I have referred more than once—a fresh and somewhat surprising approach to a familiar theme. One is the ode which opens *Music and Moonlight*:

> We are the music-makers
>   And we are the dreamers of dreams,
> Wandering by lone sea-breakers,
>   And sitting by desolate streams,

the theme being the shaping and creative effect in history of the poet's dreams. The other finds a fresh and felicitous image to express the old theme of the early, unforgotten love:

> I made another garden, yea,
>   For my new love;
> I left the dead rose where it lay,
>   And set the new above.
> Why did the summer not begin?
>   Why did my heart not haste?
> My old love came and walked therein,
>   And laid the garden waste.

But it would be idle to attempt a survey of all the lesser poets who had learned a new fashion. It is the misfortune of every fresh movement in art to beget numerous too facile, if not always infelicitous, echoes and variations. But one must not class among such echoes the work of a poet whose career ran parallel with rather than became a part of the Pre-Raphaelitic stream. Coventry Patmore chose love as the theme of his poetry and object of his devotion, and he was an artist taking a "lively pleasure in the perfection of verbal expression for its own sake." But the love of which he sings is not quite the troubled, heavy passion of Rossetti nor even the love, simpler but untroubled by thoughts of law and duty, of William Morris. *The Angel in the House* (1863) is a strangely Victorian setting and rendering of the theme set forth in the *Vita Nuova,* but the love here is not frustrated but led

on through all the episodes of an approved courtship
and duly celebrated wedding to marriage, for wedded
love is the theme of the poet's homely details and
metaphysical and religious musings. Patmore was a
Catholic too, not drawn thitherward, as far as one
may judge from his poetry, by the imaginative charm
of mediaevalism, but rather by the appeal to the in-
tellect and to his own somewhat arrogant temperament
of the fine definiteness and subtle casuistry of Catholic
theology and ethics, and the absoluteness of the
Church's authority. And to tell the truth, there
blends with Patmore's reverent devotion to woman
and to the Church a touch, a suspicion of Sir Willoughby
Patterne. Woe to the individual woman or the great
Churchman who in any way falls short of his ideals!

If in his diction and verse Patmore drew away from
Tennysonian virtuosity it was in the direction of
Wordsworthian simplicity, or even the colloquial ease
of Leigh Hunt:

> Our witnesses the cook and groom,
> We signed the lease for seven years more.

But as in Wordsworth's ballads so in Patmore's this
plainness is the ground from which in the *Preludes* and
interludes he rises to more metaphysical and imaginative flights; and Patmore's claim to a place among
lyric poets rests less on *The Angel in the House*, despite
some exquisite writing, than on the irregular odes of
The New Eros (1878), and not there most securely on
that favourite in anthologies, *The Toys*, nor the ambitious, prophetic, and political strains, but on such
great poems of love and religion as "With all my will
but much against my heart," *Tristitia*, "It was not
like your great and gracious ways," *Eurydice*, "Beautiful

habitations, auras of delight," and the combined perfection of rhythm and imagery of *Wind and Wave*.

In two directions, then, it seems to me, the wonderful stream of lyrical poetry broadened out as the century passed its middle point, when the most vital and influential of the work of Tennyson and Browning had been done—Arnold represents the feeling after a deeper strain of thought expressing itself in a simpler, severer diction, with less of virtuosity, and Patmore's very individual work may be taken as born of a similar impulse, for his very Victorian love-poetry is after all a "metaphysical" love-poetry, and into his odes he has woven, in some of them very finely, strands of Catholic theology. Of Meredith's contribution to such poetry of thought I must say a word or two later.

On the other hand, catching fire from the rich and varied virtuosity of the dramatic lyrics and idylls of Tennyson and Browning, the poets of the Pre-Raphaelitic movement had followed the direction indicated by Poe and carried still further in some ways that virtuosity, the cultivation of exotics of all kinds, exotics in sentiment and in form, the subordination of thought to sensuous beauty—suggestion and colour and music.

It remains to consider how, as the century drew towards a close, the main currents split themselves further up, like the river Oxus:

> than sands begin
> To hem his watery march, and dam his streams,
> And split his currents; that for many a league
> The shorn and parcell'd Oxus strains along
> Through beds of sand and matted rushy isles,

but narrower currents are not always the shallower.

VI

"THE NINETIES"

FROM Oscar Wilde and *The Yellow Book* there has been derived and transmitted an impression of the nineties of last century that is, to say the least, partial and misleading. To one who looks back on those years through his own memory, whatever may be his final judgment of relative values, the most startling phenomenon was, not Wilde, but Rudyard Kipling. Of Wilde, apart from factors that have nothing to do with literature, one recalls, not the poems, for such of these as have real merit come later, but the first of his brilliant essays and his *début* as a comic dramatist. Of *The Yellow Book* little lingers but the name and the drawings of Aubrey Beardsley. No; what gave distinction to the last decade of an amazing century was the emergence of a series of new poets, each with his own peculiar affinities to one or other of the great men who were passing away, but each a poet of marked individuality, a poet of distinguished achievement and promise, a promise that was or was not to be fulfilled—William Watson, Robert Louis Stevenson, Rudyard Kipling, W. E. Henley, W. B. Yeats, John Davidson, Ronald Campbell Macfie, Francis Thompson, A. E. Housman, and Thomas Hardy. I name them very much as they rise in my own memory as new experiences.

To discover, before the century ended, any unmistakable drift toward new horizons and uncharted seas would have been a difficult task. But looking back, one may discern that the trend of the new century was most clearly foreshadowed by the work of the second American poet who, after Edgar Allan Poe, has been an influence on this side of the Atlantic, Walt Whitman, and by the authors of *Barrack-Room Ballads*, *The Shropshire Lad*, and *Wessex Poems*. In their work one may study the gradual but final subsidence of the romantic wave which had traversed the century, the dislimning of those ideals, hopes, dreams, illusions, call them what you will, which had inspired a poetry of many tones and moods—the religion of Nature which "never did betray the heart that loved her," and was even for Arnold and Meredith the great consoler; the worship of Liberty which had inspired so many paeans, from Byron's to Swinburne's. The dream of the past, too, the past that never was a present, the magic of the Middle Ages, ages of Faith and also of Love, not only "affecioun of holinesse" but "love as to a creature," that too dislimns, or lingers only in a few actual or potential Catholic poets. Not any of these dreams is the theme of Whitman, of Kipling or Housman or Hardy, but the actualities of modern life. Whitman and Kipling are, indeed, still romantics, dreamers of deams, but Whitman's romance is American Democracy, Kipling's the British Empire. Mr. Housman and Thomas Hardy have no such illusions. For them, as for Leopardi,

> Amaro e noia
> La vita, altro mai nulla; e fango è il mondo.

But it is not alone the theme and the tone that changes; there is a change in the form, the technique, also. These poets have turned away from the elaborate virtuosity of so much of the poetry of the century, of which the revival at this time by Henley, Lang, and others of French forms of the fourteenth century—the rondeau, the virelay, the ballade, etc.—is the last phase, and cultivate a language "such as men do use" and simpler or more popular rhythms. Even Whitman's *vers libre* is an attempt to bring poetry into closer touch with the actualities of everyday speech. It is a strange, wheezy note is Hardy's, after the clamour and clangour of Swinburne, but has a heart-searching quality of its own.

But before I say anything of these new emergents I must touch upon two somewhat older poets who came into vogue during this decade. The publication of *Poems and Lyrics of the Joy of Earth* (1883), coinciding with the quickening of an interest in his novels, marked for many of us the first clear recognition of George Meredith as a poet of distinction and a poet strangely modern in spirit. It was hard to realise that his earliest volume dated from 1851 and had contained the first sketch of *Love in a Valley,* or that *Modern Love* had been defended and commended by Swinburne in 1862. Here it seemed to us was a new poet, a poet who did not grow musically regretful over the decay of Christian tradition and sentiment, but had

> said to the dream that caressed and the dread that smote us
> Good-night and good-bye;

and was proffering us a new reading of Earth and Man, a reading which flooded his own poetry, and the rhapsodical and imaginative pages of his novels, with a fine courage and zest of life. In Meredith's early poems his main prepossessions and habits of thought and feeling are already clear, but the style, if immature and diffuse, presents no peculiar difficulties. Not a disciple of Tennyson, he is trying in his own way after

the same kinds of effect as that poet in his earlier poems
—the sensuous, musical rendering of impressions of
Nature, of classical myths, of character, the last more
in the manner of Tennyson's dialect pieces than of
Browning in such very Meredithian poems as *The
Old Chartist* and *Juggling Jerry*. It was in his later
volumes that, as his imaginative, dramatic, analytic
power increased, there developed also the tendency to
an obscurity which is less that of Donne or Browning
than that of Chapman as described by Swinburne, the
obscurity and harshness of a poet who will insist on
singing with too many pebbles in his mouth. Wit
and imagination, the sensuous and the intellectual,
come into conflict with one another in harsh metaphors
till at times every nerve in one's body seems to protest
against these violations of the genius of the language
and its harmonies. "Donne is rugged; Jonson is stiff.
And if ruggedness of verse is a damaging blemish,
stiffness of verse is a destructive infirmity." These
words of Swinburne might be transferred from Donne
and Jonson to Browning and Meredith. The verse of
Browning may at times be harsh but it is essentially
musical. That of Meredith can be not only stiff-jointed
but flat and devoid of music:

> The godless drove unto a goal
>   Was worse than vile defeat.
> Did vengeance prick Count Louis' soul,
>   They dressed him luscious meat.

That is from a simple ballad, and one might easily
accumulate other examples from his more ambitious
poems. Of his later, longer odes, columns of smoke
lit at moments by wafts of flame, one might say, with
Swinburne again, that the reading of these poems is

"as tough and tedious a task for the mind as oakum-picking or stone-breaking for the body."

Nevertheless Meredith is a lyrical poet, moved to sing by a passionate impulse which is what distinguishes the genuine lyrical poet from the accomplished writer in lyrical form. When the wit and the thinker are controlled by the passionate imagination of the poet his song has a music of its own. If the requisites of true lyric poetry are, according to Leopardi, "inspiration or frenzy" and the perfection of "clearness and . . . simplicity, the simplicity which is really identical with naturalness, and the opposite of perceptible affectation of any kind," Meredith attained to the first, not often to the second. But he does at times, and Leopardi's clearness included the statement of the vague, what transcends mere logic and the clearness of scientific statement. Meredith's obscureness is in part the effect of the rarity and elevation of his thought. For he was in all his maturer poetry a metaphyscial poet, a poet inspired at once by his vivid sense of life and nature, and by the interpretation of their interrelation which he had derived from experience and his reading of modern science. He has two principal moods and manners. The one is grave and lofty, expressed in large, ample rhythms. Of *Modern Love* the interest is dramatic, suggesting even the comic novelist of *Evan Harrington* and *The Egoist* as in:

> we care not if the bell (*i.e.* the dinner-bell) be late;
> Though here and there grey seniors question time
> In irritable coughings.

But some of the individual sonnets are good examples of his loftiest manner, and are almost faultless poems—

the sixteenth, "In our old shipwrecked days"; the
forty-fourth, "They say that Pity in Love's service
dwells"; the forty-sixth, "At last we parley"; the
forty-seventh:

> We saw the swallows gathering in the sky,
> And in the osier-isle we heard them noise.
> We had not to look back on summer joys,
> Or forward to a summer of bright dye:
> But in the largeness of the evening earth
> Our spirits grew as we went side by side.
> The hour became her husband and my bride;

and to these add the forty-ninth and the great closing
lines of the last of the series:

> Ah, what a dusty answer gets the soul
> When hot for certainties in this our life!—
> In tragic hints see here what evermore
> Moves dark as yonder midnight ocean's force,
> Thundering like ramping hosts of warrior horse,
> To throw that faint, thin line upon the shore.

In the same large manner, grave of mood and ample
of rhythm, are composed some of the finest of his
Poems and Lyrics of the Joy of Earth and *A Reading
of Earth*, *e.g.* the best of the sonnets, the noble if
obscure *Hymn to Colour*, the closely akin *Ballad of
Past Meridian* (marred a little by the threefold repetition of "night" in the last stanza) and the finely-
mooded and cadenced *Melampus*, the most adequate
expression of Meredith's almost more than Wordsworthian sympathy with the life of nature, even the
life

> of the things
> That glide in grasses and rubble of woody wreck;
> Or change their perch on a beat of quivering wings
> From branch to branch, only restful to pipe and peck;

> Or bristled curl at a touch their snouts in a ball;
> Or cast their web between bramble and thorny hook;
> The good physician Melampus loved them all,
> Among them walked as a scholar who reads his book.

In other poems the "metaphysical" strain in Meredith's as in Donne's and some of Browning's poems, the swift passionate rush of the stream of thought, flows in swifter measures—anapaestic, trochaic four-foot lines, or, if iambic, with the heavy beat on the stressed syllables which is characteristic of the seventeenth-century "metaphysicals'" use of the Common and Long Measure. Good examples are the *Night of Frost in May, The Woods of Westermain, Hard Weather, A Faith on Trial, The Day of the Daughter of Hades.* Few of them are altogether free of the intolerable obscurities, harshnesses, and infelicities referred to earlier, but, if one has patience to win through to what the poet is trying to articulate, one gets something of the pleasurable sting derivable from the, in their different way, harsh and obscure lyrics of Donne. In the same metre as that Poet's *The Ecstasie,* Meredith's *The Thrush in February* is otherwise reminiscent of that poem:

> Since Pain and Pleasure on each hand
>   Led our wild steps from slimy rock
> To yonder sweeps of garden land,
>   We breathe but to be sword or block.
>
> The sighting brain her good decree
>   Accepts; obeys those guides, in faith,
> By reason hourly fed, that she,
>   To some the clod, to some the wraith,
>
> Is more, no mask,—a flame, a stream.
>   Flame, stream, are we in mid-career,
> From torrent source, delirious dream,
>   To heaven-reflecting current clear.

And why the sons of strength have been
  Her cherished offspring ever; how
The Spirit served by her is seen
  Through Law,—perusing love will show:

Love born of knowledge, love that gains
  Vitality as Earth it mates,
The meaning of the Pleasures, Pains;
  The Life, the Death illuminates.

For love we Earth, then serve we all;
  Her mystic secret then is ours:
We fall, or view our treasures fall,
  Unclouded, as beholds her flowers

Earth from a night of frosty wreck,
  Enrobed in morning's mounted fire,
When lowly, with a broken neck,
  The crocus lays her cheek to mire.

It was in another way than Meredith's that a
poet also older than the generation of the "nineties"
came upon us as a new experience, a poet not with a
message but with a manner, a manner that, just felt
at first, gradually penetrated the consciousness, as
might some delicate odour, with an effect at once
purifying and stimulating. It was not as a prophet
but as an artist that Robert Bridges in the *Shorter
Poems*, collected in 1894, deliberately made his appeal:
"What led me to poetry was the inexhaustible satis-
faction of form, the magic of speech lying, as it seemed
to me, in the masterly control of the material; it was
an art which I hoped to learn. I did not suppose that
the poet's emotions were in any way better than mine,
nor mine than another's." So Mr. Bridges restates
Pope's "What oft was thought but ne'er so well expressed." And the effect on those who had been
taught by Wordsworth and Tennyson and Browning
and others to think of poets as also prophets, poets

quite sure of the exceptional value of their emotions, was a twofold one. It made these beautiful poems seem, at first reading, a little wanting in interest despite their grace and naturalness of form, poems that one admires but, having laid them down, forgets to take up again. But a subsequent impression was one of relief and delight, delight in the sincerity and simplicity of the feeling, devoid of any suspicion of spasmodic violence, and in the purity and perfection of the form. After *Locksley Hall* (earlier and later), and *Pippa Passes* and *James Lee's Wife* and "two Red Roses across the Moon" and *Insomnia* and the *Song of the Bower* and "For a day and a night Love sang to us, played with us," one could, after these exaltations and complexities of emotion, find a new pleasure in the simplicity and delicate sincerity of:

> I have loved flowers that fade,
> Within whose magic tents
> Rich hues have marriage made
> With sweet unmemoried scents:
> A honeymoon delight,—
> A joy of love at sight,
> That ages in an hour:—
> My song be like a flower!
>
> I have loved airs, that die
> Before their charm is writ
> Along a liquid sky
> Trembling to welcome it:
> Notes, that with pulse of fire
> Proclaim the spirit's desire,
> Then die and are nowhere:—
>   My song be like an air!
>
> Die, song, die like a breath,
> And wither as a bloom:
> Fear not a flowery death,
> Dread not an airy tomb!

Fly with delight, fly hence!
'Twas thine love's tender sense
To feast; now on thy bier
    Beauty shall shed a tear.

Form at once so perfect and so natural repudiates the charge of virtuosity, and it is but one of many that delight by the same grace and delicacy of form if some are animated by a warmer strain of feeling: "Assemble all ye maidens at the door," "Whither, O splendid ship, thy white sails crowding," "Behold the radiant Spring," "Wherefore to-night so full of care," "Thou didst delight my eyes," "The birds that sing on autumn eves," "Beautiful must the mountains be whence ye come," and

I never shall love the snow again
            Since Maurice died:
With cornice drift it blocked the lane
And sheeted in a desolate plain
            The country side.

The trees with silvery rime bedight
            Their branches bare.
By day no sun appeared; by night
The hidden moon shed thievish light
            In the misty air.

Here and elsewhere Mr. Bridges' treatment of Nature is not quite that of any other poet. With no gospel of Nature, Wordsworthian or Meredithian, he is no mere descriptive poet. He *feels* what he portrays or suggests, witness "The north wind came up yesternight," and in irregular measures, "The storm is over, the land hushes to rest," and

Now thin mists temper the slow-ripening beams
Of the September sun,

and "In the golden glade the chestnuts are fallen all,"
and "The south wind rose at the dusk of the winter
day," and

> The lonely season in lonely lands, when fled
> Are half the birds and mists lie low, and the sun
> Is rarely seen, nor strayeth far from his bed;
> The short days pass unwelcomed one by one;

and, to take one step beyond my century, the lovely
Vignette:

> Among the meadows
>   Lightly going,
> With worship and joy
>   My heart overflowing,
>
> Far from the town
>   And toil of living,
> To a holy day
>   My spirit giving, etc.,

a poem which, with others, suggests that it is in a
qualified way one must speak of Mr. Bridges as an
artist who has no ambition to be a prophet. He has
his message for those who have ears, which is Wordsworth's and Coleridge's:

> Joy is the sweet voice, joy the luminous cloud—
>   We in ourselves rejoice!
> And thence flows all that charms or ear or sight,
>   All melodies the echo of that voice,
> All colours a suffusion from that light.

It was a strange fate that made a Poet Laureate of
Mr. Bridges, for no poet more obviously sings only
for those who have ears to hear, while a Poet Laureate
as we understand the office must attune his song also
to those whose ears are more long than sensitive. It

was an equally hard fate that prevented Sir William
Watson from occupying some such post, for no poet
of his day could have filled it more worthily. *The
Prince's Quest* (1880), indeed, a verse tale with some
lyrics interspersed, after the manner of William
Morris, which might quite fittingly have been included
in *The Earthly Paradise*, gave promise of a different
kind, of a purer, less self-conscious poetry, more
lyrical, less oratorical:

> Often when evening sobered all the air,
> No doubt but she would sit and marvel where
> He tarried, by the bounds of what strange sea;
> And peradventure look at intervals
> Forth of the window of her palace walls,
> And watch the gloaming darken fount and tree;
> And think on twilight shores, with dreaming caves
> Full of the groping of bewildered waves,
> Full of the murmur of their hollow halls.

But with the *Epigrams of Art, Life, and Nature* (1884)
and *Wordsworth's Grave and Other Poems* (1890) Mr.
Watson emerged and was hailed as the poet of public
themes and events, conscious, almost too sensitively
conscious, of his audience and the tradition of high
poetry, anxious that every poem shall appear in the
tenue correct for the occasion and the theme. As the
successor of Milton in *Lycidas* and the sonnets, of
Dryden, of Gray, of Tennyson, of Arnold in his
critical elegiac poems, Watson has done admirable
work. There are echoes in his poems, especially of
Arnold, and his thought is never strikingly original,
but *Lachrymae Musarum* is a fine piece of musical
declamation. Nor could Johnson have accused Watson
as he did Dryden, and justly, of shameless subserviency,
of being a eulogist "more delighted with the fertility

of his invention than mortified by the prostitution of his genius." Watson's poems on public themes challenged the popular prejudices of his day; his elegies on poets are clear-cut characterisations of the poet's work not unmingled with censure of current fashions and tendencies. He is the last of our great oratorical poets, his highest achievement in this kind the final section of *The Father of the Forest*. It is in song that he falls short of the highest. For even his songs leave the impression of an effect deliberately aimed at and achieved, of a peroration rather than a pure jet of song, a moment of self-revelation. Yet one of his sonnets has always left with me the feeling of such a moment of unselfconscious sincerity, *Melancholia*. The picture evoked is worthy of Dürer or suggests the Japanese print, *The Wave:*

> In the cold starlight, on the barren beach,
> Where to the stones the rent sea-tresses clave,
> I heard the long hiss of the backward wave
> Down the steep shingle, and hollow speech
> Of murmurous cavern lips, nor other breach
> Of ancient silence. None was with me save
> Thoughts that were neither glad nor sweet nor brave,
> But restless comrades each the foe of each.
> And I beheld the waters in their might
> Writhe as a dragon by some great spell curbed
> And foiled; and one lone sail; and over me
> The everlasting taciturnity;
> The august, inhospitable, inhuman night,
> Glittering magnificently unperturbed.

If Sir William Watson was the most obvious successor to the tradition of the Laureateship as Tennyson had handed it on, ennobling it in the transmission, his poetry oratorical in the dignified, classical manner of Burke and Pitt and Disraeli and Gladstone, the new

age of Imperial Democracy, of the temper which pre-
cipitated the Boer War and the oratory of the new
school of Joseph Chamberlain and Lloyd George, might
have found a suitable candidate in Rudyard Kipling.
Barrack Room Ballads (1892) was for a wide circle of
readers a much more startling eruption than any
volume of poems since the *Poems and Ballads* of
Swinburne. But if Kipling's readers and admirers
included many who were familiar with the older
volume, and recognised its influence in the new, the
circle of his admirers was a far wider one. Kipling's
new moods and measures went round the world with
the tap of the British drum. But he was a child of
his so different ancestors. He had, in fact, by birth
and education, a close link with the Pre-Raphaelites.
One of his short stories tells of a drunken soldier or
civilian (I forget which) in India who excites the sympathy and interest of the narrator by muttering in his
slumber the cadences of *The Song of the Bower:*

> Say, is it day, is it dusk in thy bower,
> Thou whom I long for, who longest for me?

and it was evident to any careful reader that the new
poet was not insensible to the music of Rossetti and
Swinburne. But Kipling was also a journalist, and
the audiences he wished to make appeal to were more
familiar with the strains of the music halls than those
of *Dolores* and *The Triumph of Time*. It was his
peculiar task to blend the popular with the more
sophisticated, and thus his favourite measures are
variations on the ballad seven and other simple rhythms,
but the rush of the anapaests and the hammer of the
trochees would not have been quite what they are if
Swinburne had not led the way. There is no imitation

but there is brilliant adaptation to a new tone and theme in:

There's a whisper down the field where the year has shot her yield,
    And the rick stands grey to the sun,
Singing "Over then, come over, for the bee has quit her clover,
    And your English summer's done."
        You have heard the beat of the offshore wind,
        And the thresh of the deep-sea rain;
        You have heard the song—how long, how long?
        Pull out on the trail again!
Ha' done with the Tents of Shem, dear lass,
    We've seen the seasons through,
And it's time to turn on the old trail, our own trail, the out trail,
    Pull out, pull out on the Long Trail—
        The trail that is always new.

And again in:

        Kabul town's by Kabul river—
          Blow the bugle, draw the sword—
        There I lef' my mate for ever,
          Wet an' drippin' by the ford.
          Ford, ford, ford o' Kabul river,
          Ford o' Kabul river in the dark!
There's the river up and brimming, an' half a squadron swimmin'
'Cross the ford o' Kabul river in the dark.

The Australian poet, Lindsay Gordon, had anticipated Kipling in the adaptation of these Swinburnian rhythms to popular strains, but in far less subtle and more imitative fashion. And it was not the rhythms alone and the felicitous use of colloquial slang, music-hall English—an extension of Wordsworth's theory that he might not have approved—but also, though without the art this would have counted for nothing, the choice of theme. That choice made him enemies, and did also tempt Kipling into facile and even vulgar excesses, cheap adventures into political propaganda. That may now be discounted, and the fact recognised that in the scattered British Empire and the British Tommy in strange lands and the British sailor in tramp steamers, Kipling had found a new, romantic, and inspiring theme. Sir Francis Doyle had to a small extent anticipated him, and Newbolt and Housman and Hardy have endorsed his discovery, in the then socially despised British Tommy, and the contact of that strange being with alien peoples and alien civilisations, one of the most romantic features in modern English life and history. But Kipling's achievement as a poet is not confined to his successes in the early ballads, *Danny Deever* and *Mandalay* and *Ford o' Kabul River* and *M'Andrew's Hymn*. As his stories have changed so have his poems, acquiring a gentler, more home-country tone and atmosphere, a purer, less journalistic art. When a careful anthology of Kipling's poems comes to be made it will be a good deal smaller than the "Inclusive Edition" of 1926, and the pride of place may be given not to the popular and ringing strains that infected our generation, if they violently repelled some readers, but to poems of a purer lyrical strain as *Puck's Song* or *Sussex* or *The Way Through the Wood*.

In the quickening of the spirit of romance and in the quest of the romantic in neglected and unexpected quarters, Kipling had allies in Stevenson and Henley, who made their *début* as poets between 1885 and 1888 and were both forces in the literary life of the nineties. But neither is a singer in the way, that despite their different faults, both Meredith and Kipling are. They are delightful writers in verse of a lyrical or semi-lyrical type. Stevenson's *Child's Garden of Verses* is a better interpretation of the average young child's moods and dreams than the *Songs of Innocence*, though it is not poetry of the same singing quality. Henley, more even than Kipling, indicated the link between journalism and poetry. His poems from those of the seventies to those of the nineties are the expression of flying impressions, but those dating from the earlier decade record the sweeter and more sentimental impressions, impressions caught from literature as well as from life. With the *In Hospital* series he becomes more consciously journalistic, choosing more realistic themes, which he continued in *London Voluntaries* and *London Types*. It would be difficult to name another poet whose work is so uniformly good of its impressionistic kind, who has yet written no single poem that quite claims a place among the best lyrics. He is pre-eminently the poet of impressions.

A greater poet of the same school was John Davidson, and it is time that justice were done to his genuine and passionate poetry. It is not perhaps entirely an accident that three poets one may fairly call "Spasmodics" were Scottish poets. It is not, I think, that an exaggerated emotionalism is typical of the Scottish character, but it is a consequence of Scottish religious thought and feeling, the stress laid upon a personal sense of sin and a sense of pardon. One has but to recall the *Letters of Samuel Rutherford* or the *Diary of Johnston of Warriston* to understand what I have in view, and the Evangelical movement of the later eighteenth and earlier nineteenth century had renewed and intensified the mood. The effect on a sensitive mind affected by the shifting currents of thought in the century was that the subject carried into his escapes and reactions the same emotional and extravagant tendencies. Alexander Smith, David Gray, Robert Buchanan, John Davidson, had all known something of the experience of which Davidson's *A Ballad in Blank Verse* is a vivid description. I have dwelt on this because I think that the best of Davidson's work is not to be found in the ballads which excited most interest on their appearance, *The Exodus from Houndsditch* and the more famous *Ballad of a Nun* and *A Ballad of Heaven*. Technically they are fine poems, the ballad measure moving with the passionate leap of Swinburne's *At a Month's End*, the imagery vivid and the inspiration sincere:

> The adventurous sun took heaven by storm;
>   Clouds scattered largesses of rain;
> The sounding cities rich and warm,
>   Smouldered and glittered in the plain.

The finest is probably *A Ballad of Heaven*, for into the tragedy and the vindication of the poor poet and dreamer Davidson put his own experience and longings:

> Listen, my love, my work is done;
>   I tremble as I touch the page,
> To sign the sentence of the sun
>   And crown the great eternal age.
>
> The slow adagio begins;
>   The winding-sheets are ravelled out
> That swathe the minds of men, the sins,
>   That wrap their rotting souls about.
>
> The dead are heralded along;
>   With silver trumps and golden drums,
> And flutes and oboes keen and strong,
>   My brave andante singing comes.

In these fine verses the overstrained note is nevertheless audible. Davidson's most enduring contribution to English lyrical poetry is not these, but his simpler, hap-

pier songs of the beauty of the country and the joys
of life—the more lyrical of the *Fleet Street Eclogues,*
earlier and later, and the nature pieces in *Ballads
and Songs* (1894). He had a pure lyric gift and should
have been a happy, not a tormented poet, driven to
rebel against an early upbringing, to contend with
poverty, and to write metaphysical testaments. In
his simpler, more sensuous poems the rhythms of
Poe and Swinburne are given a happy sweetness and
pulsation that is all his own:

> From Highbeach steepled tower
> I heard the quarter-chime—
> From the ancient and hallowed bower
> Of the beautiful virgin, Time,
> I heard the melodious vesper hour
> And the sprightly quarter-chime.
> Then the blackbird finished his song
> On a penetrant, resolute note;
> Though the thrush descanted long,
> For he knows no tune by rote—
> With sighs descanted long
> Of the sorrows he aches to tell;
> With sobs and shuddering moans,
> Like one that sings in Hell,
> He laced the phantom overtones
> Of the mellow vesper bell.
> Some terror he fain would tell
> But he never can strike the note:
> So the thrush descanted long,
> While the blackbird finished his song,
> And the woodwele's laughter ceased
> In his ashgreen gurgling throat
> On the fringe of the tone released
> By the vibrant vesper bell—
> The forest laughter ceased
> In the wake of the twilight bell,
> And high, so high from the dusky sky
> The late lark breathless fell.

Such lines from *St. Mark's Eve*, and one might continue the quotation and cite others (*e.g. Bartlemas*) from the same volume—*Holiday and other Poems* (1906)—and the seasonal songs in the first *Ballads and Songs* (1894), all these have the spontaneity and joyous flow of George Wither's lyrical rhapsodies, with a richer, more sensuous art. *A Runnable Stag* is a delightful revel of colour and rhyme. The music and pure joy of lyrical poetry is at a discount just now, but Davidson's best poems will not be ultimately lost to sight. One is more doubtful of the fate of his would-be metaphysical poems.

It was not in the realistic, journalistic direction of poems like *In Hospital, London Voluntaries, London Types, Fleet Street Eclogues, Barrack Room Ballads* that the poets to whom I referred at the beginning of this lecture, the poets who gave us the legend of the "nineties," turned for their inspiration—Oscar Wilde, Arthur Symons, Ernest Dowson, Lionel Johnson, W. B. Yeats, Francis Thompson, and some minors, whose poetry links itself in the memory, rather fancifully perhaps, with the art of Aubrey Beardsley. Their poetry is not popular in *motif* or treatment. Like their predecessors and inspirers, the Pre-Raphaelites, they are cultivators of the exotic in life and art. They have been, or some of them, loosely called "decadents," and if one accepts the late Remy de Gourmont's definition of decadence, one may so call them inasmuch as the exotic and surprising element in their poetry is found in some disassociation of ideas and sentiments which for the majority of the British public were inseparably united, established truths of thought or feeling. For even the Catholicism in which some of them found an imaginative or intellectual delight or, it

might be, an escape from themselves, is to the average
Briton something of an exotic whether he regard
it from the point of view of traditional prejudice or of
more modern "enlightenment." Mr. Yeats's sublimated
disassociation of love from the more normal "way of
a man with a maid," his strange pagan otherworldliness,
if it excited less prejudice, was quite as much of an
exotic to the many readers who could easily understand *Mandalay*. An exotic, too, for the Englishman,
bred in the tradition of Macaulay and the Whigs, was
such a poem as Lionel Johnson's *By the Statue of King
Charles at Charing Cross:*

> Our wearier spirit faints,
> Vexed in the world's employ:
> His soul was of the saints;
> And art to him was joy.

Sir William Watson, if laureated, might have been
trusted to diverge into no such heresies. His hero is
Macaulay's:

> That worn face in camps and councils bred,
> The guest who brought us law and liberty,
> Raised wellnigh from the dead.

Decadent in a more ordinary sense of the term were
the few whose disassociations brought them into dis-
astrous collision with the laws of health or with prejudices too firmly rooted to be assailed with impunity.
But my concern is with their lyrical poetry. It seems
to me that the work of three of them has the unmistakable lyrical inspiration which I have tried to
make my guiding star while selecting, as for a sketch
like this I had to do, from among many gifted, schol-
arly, and accomplished poets in every decade on which I

have so lightly touched, and these are Ernest Dowson, Francis Thompson, and William Butler Yeats. Oscar Wilde's own quest of the exotic was satisfied in his early poems by an imitative enhancement of the decorative, exotic element in the poetry of Tennyson, Keats, and the Pre-Raphaelites. He could follow Tennyson so closely as to write:

> O loved ones lying far away,
>   What words of love can dead lips send!
> O wasted dust, O senseless clay!
>   Is this the end?   Is this the end?

and imitate Arnold in a *Requiescat*. His discipleship to Rossetti and to Whistler is obvious in:

> The Thames' nocturn of blue and gold
>   Changed to a harmony of gray;
> A barge with ochre-coloured hay
>   Dropt from the wharf.

Even in the later and more justly admired, because more poignant, poems, *The Harlot's House* and the last of the sophisticated ballads of which Coleridge's is the first, one suspects or detects the influence of Dowson in the one and of Housman in the other, but *Reading Gaol*, cleared of some of its arabesques and cheap cynicism, is an arresting poem, with some verses not easily forgotten.

The final and the most poignant note of a poetry which is the expression or record of such a break with the prejudices of society or the conditions of life is that of self-pity. It is the dominant note in Wilde's ballad and in most of the few poems of Dowson. It has been said, and with some justice, that he did not write poems so much as a few delightful refrains on one or two recurrent themes—love and desire and "the days of wine and roses." The love is not very passionate. If Dowson catches at times the tone of Paul Verlaine's more wistful songs, as "C'est l'extase langoureuse" in

> Come hither, child, and rest:
> This is the end of day,
> Behold the weary west,

and if, like Verlaine, he has moments of *sagesse* and writes the *Nuns of the Perpetual Adoration:*

> Calm, sad, secure; behind high convent walls,
> These watch the sacred lamp, these watch and pray:
> And it is one with them when evening falls,
> And one with them the cold return of day,

he had, on the other hand, not the courage or else not the strength to sing the passion from which these are the reactions as Verlaine can do in a poem like *Marco:*

> Quand Marco dansait sa jupe moirée
> Allait et venait comme une marée

No; Dowson's finest poem is the subtly cadenced expression of his absorbing self-pity:

> Last night, ah, yesternight, betwixt her lips and mine
> There fell thy shadow, Cynara! thy breath was shed
> Upon my soul between the kisses and the wine;
> And I was desolate and sick of an old passion;
> Yea, I was desolate and bowed my head:
> I have been faithful to thee, Cynara! in my fashion,

a fashion on which one can make pleasing verses at any rate.

A Catholic poet, and several of these poets were Catholics, can always, in this country, be sure of a good claque, which is far better than that they should suffer from undue neglect, such as is often the fate of the less romantic Protestant. Francis Thompson's *Poems* (1893), *Sister Songs* (1895), and *New Poems* (1897) owed some of their reputation to the loyalty and enthusiasm of his friends and co-religionists. In his earliest notable lyric, *Dream Tryst*, he writes in the manner more tense than intense—as Patmore said of the older poet—of Dante Gabriel Rossetti and his school:

> The breaths of kissing night and day
> Were mingled in the eastern Heaven:
> Throbbing with unheard melody.
> Shook Lyra all its star-chord seven:
> When dusk shrunk cold, and light trod shy
> And dawn's grey eyes were troubled grey;
> And souls went palely up the sky,
> And mine to Lucidé.

It is more tense than intense because no more than in Poe's *Ulalume* can one tell exactly what it is all about, and there is something of the same tensity of feeling about lyrics like *The Daisy* and *The Poppy* where Thompson too strikes, along with that of his love for children, the musical note of self-pity:

> I hang 'mid men my needless head,
> And my fruit is dreams as theirs is bread:
> The goodly men and the sun-hazed sleeper
> Time shall reap, but after the reaper
> The world shall glean of me the sleeper.
>
> Love, I fall into the claws of Time:
> But lasts within a leaved rhyme,
> All that the world of me esteems—
> My withered dreams, my withered dreams.

The same note is played on in the longer odes, excusably in those on the more personal themes of his life and his saviours, less so in *The Dead Cardinal of Westminster*, for an ode on a public theme should at least affect a more impersonal note. But it is on his elaborate odes that the high claim made for Thompson must stand or fall. The favourite among them, *The Hound of Heaven*, is not the most elaborate but is the most passionately conceived. Structurally it opens and closes magnificently, but it is doubtful if it would lose by the omission of the third stanza where the progressive movement essential to a great ode falters; there is no clear advance in the thought; but to this ode one might allow in a measure the praise Johnson bestowed on Gray's *Elegy*. It "abounds with images which find a mirror in every mind, and with sentiments to which every bosom returns an echo"—at least every Christian bosom.

The other odes are much more deliberately, more "metaphysically" conceived, and are among the most gorgeously decorative in the language. *Sister Songs, Orient Ode, From the Night of Forebeing, Ode to the Setting Sun, An Anthem of Earth*—these get under weigh like "labouring vast Tellurian galleons," with streamers flying and high carved poops, majestic of movement if at times answering a little uncertainly to the helm. Thompson was well read and does not hesitate to adopt or adapt phrases and images and rhythms from Donne and Crashaw and Spenser and Shelley and Wordsworth and Coleridge and Edgar Allan Poe; but he took two poets as his models in the ode—Crashaw for sentiment and style, "sowing with the sack rather than with the hand," and Coventry Patmore in construction, affecting at times, but not very convincingly, that poet's haughty temper. Each ode is, like Patmore's, the elaboration of a thought—

metaphysical, religious. *By Reason of Thy Law* is a
slightly different rendering of the older poet's *Remembered Grace*, a little more personal in reference.
But Thompson's thought is set forth with a wealth
of description and imagery and hyperbole that is very
different from Patmore's dignified, sinewy style. He is
a great rhetorician, a *rhétoriqueur*, reviving or coining
words, accumulating imagery more deliberately sensuous than that of Keats, more industriously learned
than that of Donne. His Nature imagery is more
gorgeous than sensitive. His descriptions are richly-
coloured canvases, like the historical pictures of Mr.
Abbey. They never give you the authentic thrill of
some of Meredith's readings or Bridges' "The north
wind came up yesternight." "The country was never
his true home nor did he ever learn to distinguish the
oak from the elm." His descriptions are decorative
and ritualistic:

> Lo, in the sanctuaried East,
> Day, a dedicated priest,
> In all his robes pontifical exprest,
> Lifteth slowly, lifteth sweetly,
> From out its Orient tabernacle drawn,
> Yon orbed sacrament confest,
> Which sprinkles benediction through the dawn;
> And when the grave procession's ceased,
> The earth with due illustrious rite
> Blessed,—ere the frail fingers featly
> Of twilight violet-cassocked acolyte
> His sacerdotal stoles unvest—
> Sets for high close of the mysterious feast,
> The sun in exposition meetly
> Within the flaming monstrance of the West.

That is not entirely characteristic, for Thompson's
imagery is often more paganly riotous but it does well

illustrate the almost painful elaboration of his art, its exotic flavour—and it does also show what was his great endeavour in these poems, to combine the nature worship of the poets he loved with Catholic thought and sentiment, a difficult task. If Thompson's odes fall short of complete success it is because he has failed to integrate the poetic vesture and the thought. We can grasp the main thought and admire, more or less wholeheartedly, the rich imagery and rhythms, but the two are not quite made one even in so fine an ode as *To the Setting Sun*. He comes perhaps nearer in *The Night of Forebeing* where the underlying theme becomes, as in Shelley's *Ode to the West Wind*, the poet's own sorrow and aspiration.

"I was in all things Pre-Raphaelite," Mr. Yeats tells us, and of his friend and master, Henley, he says: "I disliked his poetry because he wrote in *vers libre* and filled it with unimpassioned description of an hospital ward. . . . I wanted the strongest passions that had nothing to do with observation, sung in metrical forms that seemed old enough to be sung by men half asleep or riding upon a journey." Later he tells us: "Though I went to Sligo every summer I was compelled to live out of Ireland . . . and was but keeping my mind upon what I knew must be the subject-matter of my poetry." All that Mr. Yeats tells us of his own development, by far the fullest and most interesting of any of the group, is not easy to follow, but the quotations suggest what seem to an outsider the main sources of his work. He had no desire to sing the actualities of modern life. "Art for Art's sake" was his Pre-Raphaelitic motto; rhetoric and didactic have ever been his bugbears. But the Pre-Raphaelites introduced him to Blake, and it was not for nothing that he edited that poet, if editing demands more of "observation" than a poet is always willing to give. From Blake he learned and accepted as fundamental the opposition of the reason and the imagination:

> Beloved, gaze in thine own heart,
>   The holy tree is growing there;
> From joy the holy branches start,
>   And all the trembling flowers they bear.

But

> Gaze no more in the bitter glass
>   The demons, with their subtle guile,
> Lift up before us when they pass,
>   Or only gaze a little while,
>
> . . . .
>
> The glass of outer weariness
> Made when God slept in days of old.

Whether indeed Mr. Yeats's was a more passionate lover than the author of *Hawthorn and Lavender* we need not discuss. The love of his earlier poems is undoubtedly a more sublimated, ethereal, imaginative passion, more akin than was that of Rossetti to the love which inspires the sonnets of Dante and Petrarch, because like theirs an unfulfilled passion. This is the theme of the loveliest of his carefully and delicately wrought lyrics, *The Rose of the World*, *The Sorrow of Love*, "When you are old and gray and full of sleep," *The White Birds*, *To an Isle in the Water*, all in the *Poems* of 1899, and *A Poet to His Beloved*, in *The Wind among the Reeds*. The latter volume is by the initiated considered the best of his early works, but the passion here is almost too ethereal for the normal reader. To my mind, the fullest expression of this love, that longs but is never fulfilled, is the *Baille and Aillinn* and *Adam's Curse* of the 1905 volume. In these poems and all his work, Mr. Yeats has cultivated simplicity of diction and order of words with as much ardour and labour as Thompson devoted to his decorations. But it is a sophisticated simplicity, for the contrast between the apparent ease and naturalness of the style and the subtlety and elusiveness of what is said is often quite startling. For his study of Blake and of Irish mythology complicated his love-poetry. From Blake he learned the metaphysical interpretations of this interval between longing and fulfilment, viz. the illusoriness of the world of the senses, the fulfilment of desire in a world that lies behind the veil:

> When the mortal eyes are closed,
> And cold and pale the limbs reposed.

But Blake's dream of the world behind the sensible is derived from Christianity and Swedenborg; Mr. Yeats turned to the traditions of old Celtic legend. "If," says the late Professor Ker, "the imagination of the Northern mythologists was dominated by the thought of the fall of the gods, the day when Odin meets with the wolf, the Celts have given their hearts to the enchanted ground, to the faëry magic, in many stories of adventures in the underworld and voyages westward to an island paradise." Accordingly Yeats's other world has no hint of the Christian elements of benevolence and innocence of Blake's:

> The pleasure which unsought falls around the infant's path,
> And on the fleeces of mild flocks who neither care nor labour.

Yeats's other world, of whose entrancing joys Niamh and other beings, strange to the English mind, sing, has only one activity and that is love. There lovers wander:

> Murmuring softly lip to lip,
> Murmuring gently how far off are the unquiet lands;

and of Baille and Aillinn, who died brokenhearted, we
hear that:

> This young girl and this young man
> Have happiness without an end,
> Because they have made so good a friend.
> They know all wonders, for they pass
> The towery gate of Gorias,
> And Findrias and Falias,
> And long-forgotten Murias,
> Among the giant kings whose hoard,
> Cauldron and spear and stone and sword,
> Was robbed before the earth gave wheat;
> Wandering from broken street to street
> They come where some huge watcher is,
> And tremble with their love and kiss.

Dwelling on these Irish legends and on the charm of
traditional spoken poetry Mr. Yeats was attracted by the
thought of composing himself poems of the same popu-
lar kind. He wrote a few quite simple songs and ballads,
The Lake Isle of Innisfree (his most popular song),
When You are Old, *A Dream of a Blessed Spirit*, *The
Stolen Child*, and *The Ballad of Molly Magee*, *The
Ballad of Father Hart*, *The Ballad of the Foxhunter*.
Even in these there are touches alien to the genuine
popular song or ballad, and in his more characteristic
The Happy Townland and "I went out to the hazel
wood" the effect is one of extreme sophistication:

> The little fox he murmured,
> "O what of the world's bane?"
> The sun was laughing sweetly,
> The moon plucked at my rein;
> But the little red fox murmured,
> "O do not pluck at his rein,
> He is riding to the town-land
> That is the world's bane."

The quest of the exotic could hardly go farther. Mr.

Yeats's poetry has grown increasingly subtle and sophisticated, though the tone has in some remarkable ways altered. It has become more enigmatical, if less dreamy. But this later poetry, intellectual, and enigmatic, full of memories and regrets, regrets as of one who feels that he sacrificed too much to "the old high way of love" and now reproaches, not as a Ronsard, his mistress, but himself, and would even, by touches of harsh realism, avenge himself a little on the dreamer of the early poems, this hardly belongs to my theme but to the critic of more recent poetry. The most beautiful and poignant—*Fallen Majesty, Friends, The Cold Heaven, No Second Troy, Reconciliation, The Wild Swans of Coole, Solomon to Sheba, Her Praise, Leda and the Swan,* and others are on old themes if the art has grown more masculine.

It is impossible in a short compass to touch on all the phases of the final ebullience of the lyrical spirit of the century in this its last decade. In the same year as *Barrack Room Ballads* appeared a small volume which passed in the main unnoticed but whose genuine lyrical inspiration caught the quick eye of Saintsbury and Lang and John Addington Symonds. Unfortunately Macfie's *Granite Dust* (1892) was not followed up till 1904, when the tide was setting in a new direction, and his poetry has never had its full due. Like other Scottish poets he is somewhat of a Spasmodic and shares their predilection for preaching. He is, too, like a good singer who occasionally sings flat. But the sincere passion, the purity and unsophisticated simplicity of style, and the music of verse are those of a true lyrical poet, not an accomplished writer in lyrical forms. No unprejudiced reader can fail to enjoy in *Granite Dust,—With a Gift of Roses, The*

Dying Day of Death, and some shorter pieces, and in the *New Poems* of 1905 the fine ode: "If I were Sleep." To these should be added two other finely builded odes, *The Titanic* and *War.*

But I must say a word in closing on the two poets who sang the swan-song of the century, its faiths and hopes and dreams. *A Shropshire Lad* (1896) came upon us in the nineties, not yet grown familiar with blasphemy, angry or flippant, as the present generation has, like an explosive, stinging shell. Mr. Housman has but one theme, and his insistence, in poem after poem, does just a little recall Carlyle's story of the traveller at an inn who laid down his knife and fork at intervals to exclaim in tones of eloquent woe, "I've lots my a-a-a-appetite"; but the poet has expressed his loss of appetite for life, his Swiftian anger with all that makes it bitter—the unhappy course of true love, the grim shadow of approaching death, it may be on the gallows—with a concision and perfection of form worthy of the Greek Anthology. His measures are of the simplest—Long Measure, Common or Ballad Measure, and Alexandrines, the last generally divided into three and three. But occasionally as his strain rises he uses a longer and more plangent line, or runs the two sections of the Alexandrine more closely together:

> Be still, my soul, be still; the arms you bear are brittle.
>   Earth and high heaven are fixed of old and founded strong.
> Think rather, call to mind, if now you grieve a little,
>   The days when we had rest, O soul, for they were long,

and in the *New Poems* (1922), "The chestnut casts his flambeaux, and the flowers," and, in seven-foot lines, the passionate poem, " 'Tis mute the word they went to hear on high Dodona mountain," and again, "West and away the wheels of darkness roll," and finally the epitaph, *On An Army of Mercenaries*, the finest composed since Simonides wrote his upon the fallen at Thermopylae. The passionate sincerity of the feeling redeems its monotony, and that is further relieved by the beautiful interwoven embroidery of English scenery, and the dramatic art that puts these sentiments into the mouth of simple English men and soldiers. Could anything be more perfect than, to take a casual example, the poem which opens:

> Far in a western brookland
> That bred me long ago
> The poplars stand and tremble
> By pools I used to know,

and ends:

> There, by the starlit fences,
> The wanderer halts and hears
> My soul that lingers sighing
> About the glimmering weirs.

In that, as in all of Mr. Housman's short poems, it would be impossible to change a word without injury to the perfectly chosen but unobtrusive epithets, without injury to the subtly interwoven alliteration.

It was no such concise perfection of statement that appealed to us in *Wessex Poems* (1898), in which the same *motif* of impatience with a world where

> Crass casualty obstructs the sun and rain,
> And dicing Time for gladness casts a moan,

is played upon in a greater variety of tones of which the dominant is rather pity than anger, and anger when it appears is more querulous than savage. It was a strange impression that a reader, familiar with Hardy's novels, derived from turning over the pages of this unexpected volume. This must be, one thought, an experiment in a form not quite familiar to the writer, but that was contradicted by the dates. One can recall reading one poem after another, wondering at the awkward movement of the verse in the ballads, the strange use of certain words as by one who was more intent upon what he had to say than disposed to let the words dictate their own usage:

> Along through the Stour-bordered Forum
> Where Legions had wayfared,
> And where the slow river-face glasses
> Its green canopy,
>
> And by Weatherby Castle, and thencefrom
> Through Casterbridge held I
> Still on, to entomb her my mindsight
> Saw stretched pallidly.

One was not used to such rhythms then, though I suppose they are common enough today. And then one came upon Drummer Hodge and one thrilled, for here was an effect not sentimental but authentically imaginative; and so other lyrics asserted themselves, *Friends Beyond, In a Wood, The Impercipient,* and others including some of the ballads; and all that followed the appearance of the first volume has only deepened without much altering the first impression. One reads always with a certain latent protest against these somewhat laboured and wheezy rhythms, the occasionally awkward, even ugly words:

> Where once she domiciled.

and yet lyric after lyric justifies itself and lingers in

the memory in virtue of the clear statement of the poet's feeling, and the depth, the beauty, and the absolute sincerity of that feeling—*The Darkling Thrush, Beyond the Last Lamp, The Going,* "Only a man harrowing clods," *The Night of Trafalgar,* and many others. In contrast with the author of *The Shropshire Lad,* Hardy experimented in a great variety of metres and stanza forms. There is always a slightly wheezy note in the music, but there *is* music and that, like the choice of theme and the diction, always Hardy's own. It would be difficult to find sources or parallels for such rhythms as

> Farmer Dewy, Tranter Reuben, Farmer Ledlow, late at plough,
> Robert's kin and John's and Ned's,
> And the Squire and Lady Susan, lie in Melstock churchyard now!

and

> While rain, with eve in partnership,
> Descended darkly, drip, drip, drip,
> Beyond the last low lamp I passed
> Walking slowly, whispering sadly,
> Two linked loiterers, wan, downcast:
> Some heavy thought constrained each face,
> And blinded them to time and place,

but he owes something, it seems to me, of suggestion at any rate, in his rhythms and stanzas, to a beautiful lyrist of an earlier decade—the Dorsetshire poet William Barnes, whose first dialect pieces appeared as early as 1842 and the collected *Poems of Rural Life in the Dorset Dialect* in 1879. For Hardy was deeply read in, and an ardent lover of, the romantic poetry of the century from Shelley to Swinburne. His lyrics on other poets are interestingly different from Watson's; no effort at a critical estimate, but intensely personal statements of the romantic appeal made to his own imagina-

tion by the life and the poetry of Shelley and Keats, by
the splendours of *Poems and Ballads*. And there is a
significance in his feeling for these poets. With all
his realism, his distrust of the dreams of the century,
his poetry of the truth as he sees it, and of his own
reactions to the facts of life, there is a suppressed
romanticism in Hardy's poetry of life and nature. His
heart and imagination are on the side of the dreamers
from Blake to Wordsworth and Shelley and Keats to
Swinburne and Meredith, if his sensitiveness to experience and to the thought of his day make him a poet,
but a wistful poet, of disillusionment. His minor-
keyed poetry and its hesitating music is a strange but
not entirely inappropriate close to the ardours and
aspirations and dreams and joys and sorrows and all
the manifold virtuosity of what is, when all is said,
the greatest century in the history of English lyrical
poetry. It is so in virtue both of its content and
the rich variety of the form it has taken. I have
used the word "metaphysical" more than once, and
that because the seventeenth century has given to the
word, in relation to poetry, a somewhat different
meaning from "philosophical"; suggests, not so much
a cold, lofty poetry of systematic thought, like that of
Lucretius in parts, or of Sir Fulke Greville, or of
Leconte de Lisle, but a poetry in which thought and
passion are in a strange way blended. But the metaphysical poetry of the seventeenth century begins and
ends, in truth, with Donne and some of his religious
disciples. The sharp separation between the secular
and the devout of that epoch prevented the metaphysical poetry of love which Donne inaugurated being
further developed. The love-poetry of his successors
degenerated into conceit and cynicism. The century

of Metaphysical lyric was the nineteenth. Never has there been put into poetry, lyrical or rhapsodical, such a wealth of passionate thinking about life and nature and love (Browning, Patmore, Rossetti, Morris, Swinburne, Yeats), and liberty, and justice, and the past, and the future—yes, and about art and poetry themselves—as in this period when poetry kept, to its honour, in such close touch with the movement of science and philosophy and religious feeling and social upheavals, whether in sympathy with them, or in reaction against them and passionate protest against their apparent implications. And not less remarkable than the variety and wealth of thought and feeling was the development of the form in which these found expression. Blake unconsciously, and Coleridge more understandingly, had emancipated English metre from the bondage of the iambic rhythm which is not its natural rhythm. "English unforced metre," says that sound critic Mr. Kellet, *"naturally* runs in trips and so-called anapaests; the *regular* succession of iambics and trochees is only attained by some degree, more or less pronounced, of violence." Or one may say with Professor Legouis that English lyrical verse always tends to reassert the old English principle of stress rather than the regular syllabism which we borrowed from the French. Of lyrical measures thus emancipated Coleridge and Shelley and Tennyson and Swinburne developed probably every possible variety and subtlety, so that questors for something new have perforce turned in the direction either of *vers libre* or the cultivation of syllabic quantity. But into the questions raised by more modern poetry, Georgian or other, it would be dangerous, and at the close of a volume impossible adequately to enter. "There is no

such thing, cry the new school" (so Mr. Rylands
boasts) "as an unpoetical subject; and they have the
Elizabethans on their side." That may well be, but
the statement cuts both ways. To despise the Victorians for fleeing from life, whatever that may mean,
or if it be true, and resolving that *we* shall not do so,
will not make us greater poets. That will depend on
how we treat our new themes. A great poetry will
not come from preferring *Waste Land* to the *Ode
to a Nightingale,* because it chooses a more un-
promising theme. It will depend on the genius of the
poets and, I venture to think, on their being sustained and inspired by some ardour of faith or conviction such as gave us romantic poetry. If "the
eighteen-nineties caused an explosion of laughter," one
knows not with what rueful eye the generations to
come may contemplate their successors. On all human
ventures the eye of philosophy will look with mixed
feelings:

> Meanwhile on him, her chief
> Expression, her great word of life, looks she;
> Twi-minded of him, as the waxing tree,
> Or dated leaf.

Whether Georgian and later poetry be the waxing tree
or the dated leaf remains for a later history to show.